Titus Smith 1768 – 1850
By Craig Balzer 2017

Exploring Paradise

Nova Scotia
In
1801-1802

The journals of Titus Smith

SURVEY,

Of the Eastern and Northern Parts Of the Province.

In the Years 1801 & 1802.

With General Observations thereon.

ALSO, A SURVEY

Of the Lands between

Sackville (Bedford) and Shubenacadie.

And observations on the

Western Parts of the Province.

With a list of trees, shrubs, grasses, and plants.

And observations on the nature and uses of the trees

By Titus Smith jr

HALIFAX

1857

INTRODUCTION

The Nova Scotia Provincial Archives microfilm collection contains at least three versions of the journals of Titus Smith. There is the original, which appears to be a small notebook of hundreds of pages; a handwritten copy of the Northern and Eastern tours from 1857, calling itself the 3rd edition "Written from the original in the Possession of James Irons by Rob't. Jas. Wilson"; and a typewritten copy, which I used as the source for this transcription. Being thrice removed from the original, there are bound to be errors. I've checked the spelling and reformatted some of the tables, but it will require someone with more patience than I to compare this now digital version with the original.

In addition, there exists a typed transcription of the journal entries focusing on forestry. This was done by Lloyd S. Hawboldt, a forester of the Nova Scotia Department of Lands and Forests in 1955 and is in the Natural Resources library.

I think the history and location of the journals is complicated, but I haven't tracked them very carefully. I am just grateful to find them in one place.

Included here, by way of introduction to Titus, is a lengthy essay by Harry Piers. I think the title "THE DUTCH VILLAGE PHILOSOPHER" is not quite right for 21st century ears. Smith was what we would now call a scientist, most especially a botanist and geologist. He had an encyclopedic knowledge of Linnaeus, who had only died in 1778. He seems well acquainted with rocks and minerals.

Wikipedia says: From the ancient world, starting with Aristotle, to the 19th century, the term "natural philosophy" was the common term used to describe the practice of studying nature. Isaac Newton's book Philosophiae Naturalis Principia Mathematica (1687), whose title translates to "Mathematical Principles of Natural Philosophy", reflects the then-current use of the words "natural philosophy", akin to "systematic study of nature".

There are lots of threads to Titus' story – a connection to the short stay of the Maroons, his interest in the history of the province, his mentoring of Maria Morris Miller – but his three tours are most remarkable.

May 1801 was three years before Lewis and Clark explored the American West and in a real sense the interior of Nova Scotia was equally uncharted. Although never far from settlements on the coast, Smith's long and difficult trek was into unknown and unexplored territory. One article (Clark) estimates the population of Nova Scotia at about 50,000 at the time.

Included here, after the journals, is Smith's long letter in the 1835 Magazine of Natural History (London). It provides some insight into his observations and theories. His comments on forest succession and plant associations ring pretty true, but his discussion of 'aerial fluid' is more speculative. To me, it sounds a lot like he's describing carbon dioxide.   A modern science historian could elaborate on the context.

Another article is worth reading:

> Titus Smith, Junior, and the Geography of Nova Scotia in 1801 and 1802 by Andrew H. Clark. Published in the Annals of the Association of American Geographers, Vol. 44, No. 4 (Dec., 1954), pp. 291-314

Clarke is the source of the maps in the Nova Scotia Archives, reproduced here. His article focuses on the journals as historical geography, offering a summary and synthesis of the tours. It is not included here, but may be purchased from JSTOR for $9.99.

And yet another:

Titus Smith, A Pioneer of Plant Ecology in North America by Eville Gorham is published in Ecology, Vol. 36, No. 1 (Jan., 1955), pp. 116-123

is also available on JSTOR

In fact, there is a lot of material on Titus. The primary sources are widely scattered – up to now, the journals have been a noticeable gap. I hope their publication will revive interest in Titus the scientist.

A couple of details:

I've omitted the very short (1 page, no map) "Survey of the Lands Between Sackville and Shuben-Acadie".

When it seemed warranted, I've kept Smith's spelling and capitalization. The exuberant use of capitals in the Western Tour is pretty faithful to the typed transcript.

An abiding mystery has been Smith's constant use of "Tremain's Brook" and "F.W." to gauge the size of streams. I still don't know where Tremain's is, but F.W. is Fresh Water Brook, which is the now buried watercourse that runs through the Public Garden in Halifax.

Warren Reed

Halifax

2017

COMPANION WEBSITE

This book has a companion website at:

https://titussmithns.blogspot.com/

There you can download KML and image files for use in Google Earth, allowing you to

- Read the journals within the context of a map
- Fly along the course Smith describes
- Make movies of tours
- Set the background to include or exclude contemporary infrastructure and photos
- Make measurements and explore areas close up
- Overlay original maps of Smith's travels

In addition, there is an opportunity to link to other sources, make corrections, leave comments and suggest further uses for the information. Please join the conversation.

Be creative! Find a campsite from 1801 and take pictures, check Titus' geology, tell us about people he mentions, tell your own story......

My fondest hope is that people will use Titus as a jumping off point to explore this wonderful province, its history, its Natural History and the people who made it what it is today.

Hello Mr. Reed,

Thank you for having contacted the Nova Scotian Institute of Science to request permission to reproduce in your upcoming publication the following monograph:

Piers, Harry. 1938. *Titus Smith, "The Dutch Village Philosopher," Pioneer Naturalist of Nova Scotia, 1768-1850. Halifax, N.S.: Nova Scotian Institute of Science.*

On behalf of the Nova Scotian Institute of Science, I consulted with Roger Gillis, the Dalhousie University Copyright Librarian about author rights. The monograph's author Harry Piers died 77 years ago (in 1940), which means that copyright on the monograph has expired and that it is in the public domain. You do not need permission to reproduce the booklet.

As a member of the Council of the Nova Scotian Institute of Science (NSIS), I have communicated your request and intentions to the President Sherry Niven and fellow councilors. NSIS thanks you for alerting the Institute to your plan to reproduce the Titus Smith monograph in your book and wishes you well in your endeavour. Your book will no doubt renew public interest in Titus Smith and perhaps in Harry Piers as well, the latter having been President of NSIS during the 1930s.

Best wishes,

Michelle Paon

NSIS Librarian

Table of Contents

Harry Piers

TITUS SMITH
"THE DUTCH VILLAGE PHILOSOPHER"
PIONEER NATURALIST OF NOVA SCOTIA, 1768-1850.

By Harry Piers, Curator of the Provincial Museum, Halifax, N.S.

(Part of a presidential address delivered before the N.S. Institute of Science, 14th Oct., 1936.)

This paper has been prepared in order to preserve a record of the life and accomplishments of an unusually remarkable man who, as far as I know, was the first scientific naturalist in Nova Scotia and therefore may be called the Father of Natural Science in this province. I refer to that old worthy, Titus Smith, who has now been dead for eighty-six years. It is a mere act of justice to recall what he accomplished since he turned his attention to the study of nature nearly a century and a half ago, and to thereby help keep his memory green – for I fear that he whose name was once on everyone's lips here, is now forgotten.

Titus Smith was born at Granby, a small village in Hampshire Co., Massachusetts, about ten miles north-northeast of Springfield, on 4 September, 1768, [1] being the eldest child of the Rev. Titus Smith by his wife, Damaris, daughter of Aaron Nash of Granby, to whom he had been married in the previous year. He died at the Dutch Village, near Halifax, N.S., on 4 January, 1850.

Titus Smith, Senr.

In order to better understand the atmosphere surrounding the early life of the main subject of this sketch, and to know the remarkable character and eventful career of the parent under whose capable care he was raised and educated, we must first devote some attention to the elder Titus.

He was born at South Hadley, Mass., on 4 or 23 June, 1734, and died at the Dutch Village, near Halifax, N.S., on 15 September, 1807, at the age of seventy-three. He was the fourth child of Select-man 'Deacon' John Smith (b. 1697), who was a son of 'Orphan' John Smith (1665-1724), son of John Smith (1637 ? -76), son of Lieut. Samuel Smith (1602-80) who had come in the ship 'Elizabeth' of Ipswich from Old to New England in the spring of 1634, only fourteen years after the landing of Pilgrim Fathers. During the French War he spent two years, 1756-57. as a volunteer fighting the frontier Indians in what is now New York State, in which war his

---

1 His brother, William, gives the year as 1769; but Mrs. Lawson (on the authority of W.A. Hendry), Mrs. E.M. Cole, a descendant, and Dr. F.B. Dexter, in his Biographical Sketches of Yale Graduates, all give the year as 1768, which is no doubt correct. The inscription on Smith's monument says he died Jan. 4, 1850, aged 81 years, which helps to confirm it.

brother so distinguished himself as a scout that it is claimed he was the original of 'Hawkeye' in Cooper's 'The Last of the Mohicans' (1862).

On his return from the frontier, Titus, whose constitution was not strong, entered Yale College, New Haven, from which he graduated in 1764. In the following winter he went to the Rev. Mr. Wheelock's Indian Charity School at Lebanon, Conn., to learn the Indian language; in March he was approved, by the Scottish society under which Wheelock was working, as one of its missionaries to the Indians; and on 24 April, he and his life-long Yale friend, Theophilus Chamberlain, were ordained, no doubt as Congregational ministers, by the Rev. Solomon Williams and others. In June they went to the territory of the Six-Nations Indians in New York Province, establishing themselves first at Oneida and then at Onohoquaga (now Colesville, Broome Co.). Their work was hampered by rival missions of the Society for the Propagation of the Gospel; and later Smith returned home. Ill health prevented his resuming his missionary labours.

For a short while he presided over a small church in the village of West Suffield, Conn.; and it was at North Suffield, in 1767, he married a lady whom he had been engaged for seven years, Damaris (b. 19 Nov., 1737, d. Aug., 1779), eldest child of Aaron and Damaris (Waite) Nash of his native village. It was at Granby that his first child, Titus, was born. For some years, while having his home at Granby, he went about as an itinerant preacher, often holding forth in an open field before an audience of many thousands. Then, because of diseased lungs and liver he had to cease preaching. Thereupon he took up the study of medicine with such energy as his health permitted. He was also an enthusiastic amateur botanist and skillful mathematician and chemist, and corresponded with the natural philosopher, Dr. Joseph Priestly (1733-1804), although this may not have been until the latter's removal to America in 1794.

He, like many others in New England, had become profoundly impressed by the appealingly simple theological tenets of Dr. John Glas (1695-1773) and his son-in-law, Robert Sandeman (1718-71), as set forth in their writings which were then agitating the Church of Scotland. It is difficult to state just when he became imbued with their beliefs and joined the Sandemanian Church, to which belonged many of the most influential of the later Boston and Connecticut Loyalists. I would certainly have expected it to have been about 1768, but that his son, William (b. 1777), says that his father opened a correspondence with Sandeman whom he induced to come to New England, that is in 1764. At the least we know that previous to 1772, and probably in 1768 when his friend T. Chamberlain was similarly appointed, he was re-ordained at Boston as an Elder, or unpaid minister, in the Sandemanian Church. That sect never sanctioned a paid clergy, so that its elders had to gain a living by secular employment.

A notable Sandemanian Church had been founded at Danbury, Conn., the place of Sandeman's abode, and there Smith moved. His son says that Sandeman died at his father's house there in April, 1771, but Dr. Dexter says he died at the home of T. Chamberlain. It is quite possible that Smith and Chamberlain lived in the same house.

On the outbreak of the American War of Independence in 1775. Smith sympathized to some extent with the revolting colonies; but his benign religion having taught him to submit to established authority, he, like practically every Sandemanian, sided with the Royalists. Washington, hearing of his knowledge of chemistry, appealed to him to make gunpowder for his men, but this he refused to do.

In April or May, 1777, Danbury was burnt by the British Hessian troops, and it was probably then that he went to New Haven, where his home was frequently visited by men of letters. Late in that year, he with others of his co-religionists joined in signing a memorial setting forth their inability, because of religious scruples, to join in active opposition to the King's government. As a result, by an Act of the Assembly, the signers were obliged to leave New Haven.

He took refuge within the British lines at Bushwick, Long Island, opposite to New York. There his wife, Damaris, died in Aug., 1779, in her forty second year, leaving him with three sons and daughter, of whom the eldest, Titus, was but eleven years of age.[2] Subsequently he married Lydia Barstow, by whom he had no children.

On the British evacuation of New York in the latter part of 1783, Smith and his family came with many other Loyalists, including Theophilus Chamberlain, to Halifax, Nova Scotia; and in October of the next year (1784) he became one of the most prominent of the original Loyalist grantees of the new Township of Preston near Dartmouth. His land was apparently where 'Riverbank', the Silver estate, is now situated, between the tracts granted to Theophilus Chamberlain and to George Westphal, a retired officer of the recently disbanded Hessian troops and father of two British admirals. It was on the north side of the Old Preston Road, just west of Little Salmon River, a locality which is now called Westphal. There he and his family built a house and began the hard work of clearing a farm.

As there were numerous Sandemaninans among the earlier Boston (1776) and later New York Loyalists, and they had founded a church at Halifax, Smith ministered to them as an Elder, that sect, as we have said, having no regular paid clergy. All of his children, except Titus, Jr., returned to Litchfield, Conn., about 1795; although one, Sylvester (born 1773), came back before 1800, settled on the north side of

---

[2] His children were: (1) Titus, born at Granby, Mass., in 1768; (2) Rebekah (afterwards Mrs. Richardson of Litchfield, Conn.), born at Danbury, Conn., 1771; (3) Sylvester, born at Danbury, 1773, died near Dartmouth, N.S.; and (4) William, born at New Haven, Conn., 1777.

the Preston Road, a little west of the old York house, nearly two and a half miles from Dartmouth, married, probably about 1806, Hester Wisdom, sister of the wife of his brother Titus, had a family of nine sons and one daughter, [3] and finally, when in the prime of life, died as the result of having been gored by Alex. Farquharson's bull in Farquharson's pasture near Smith's home. He was a carpenter by trade, was poetically inclined, and being familiar with the Greek and Latin languages, made for amusement translations from Homer, and also wrote Latin verse.

Titus Smith, Junr.

Having given this necessary account of the father, which illustrates the remarkable character of that man and the stirring and changing circumstances under which his children were reared; we will hereafter devote ourselves mainly to the career of the primary subject of this sketch, his eldest child, Titus, afterwards known as the 'The Dutch Village Philosopher'. As we have seen, his childhood had been spent with his father in Granby, Mass., in Danbury and New Haven, Conn., and near New York, where in 1779 he had been left motherless.

As to his education, we find that at very early age he had the advantage of careful teaching of his talented and studious father, and he also attended a private school at New Haven kept by another Yale graduate and Sandemaninan adherent named Daniel Humphreys (1740-1827). His progress was very rapid. At four years of age (1772) he could read English books with ease, at seven (1775) had gained considerable proficiency in Latin, while at twelve (1780) he could translate the most difficult writers in that language,

---

[3] Sylvester's eldest child, Henry Smith (1807?-1891?), lived in Dartmouth and in Halifax, and married Catharine Munroe (1817-1907), daughter of Henry Munroe, who was son of Lt. Col. Henry Munroe, M.P.P., of Annapolis Co. Sylvester's youngest child, Stephen, wrote poetry, and lived at Marlborough, near Boston, Mass.

and also had made good progress in Greek. Furthermore, he was studying German and French. It was the constant practice in his father's family for one to read aloud while the others listened; and when the book was in Latin, Greek or French, young Titus was always selected as the reader. Unlike other children, he had no desire to join in their usual amusements, but sought the society of those from whom he might derive knowledge.

When his father came to Nova Scotia he was a lad of fifteen years, and under the guidance of his parent he continued to read the classics, and also devoted increasing time to the study of plant-life which, as we have said, was a favourite study of the elder Smith. He also became attached to the study of mathematics and astronomy, in which he gained some proficiency. Apart from all this, he and his brothers cheerfully assisted their father in the necessary and more utilitarian labour of felling timber, clearing stubborn land, building notably good stone-walls, and planting, cultivating and harvesting crops whereby they made a scanty living.

About 1790 or 1791 John Wentworth (afterwards Lieut. Governor) presented to the elder Titus a complete set of the botanical works of the great Linnaeus (1707-78). From that time the young man devotes much of the flowering season to intensive botanical studies. Later he also read other works such as Christian Hendrik Person's 'Synopsis Plantarum' published at Paris, 1805-7. With the scientific investigation of plants, the Smiths also gave much attention to more practical matters associated therewith, and they had a special plot in their well-kept garden, which was devoted to experimental work in agriculture, horticulture and floriculture, as mentioned by Lieut. John Clarkson in his Journal for 12 October, 1791 (see Coll. N.S. Hist. Soc., vol. 7, p. 139). We may readily recognize the elder Smith as Clarkson's 'honest gardener' and 'excellent botanist'. Some contributions made by the father to the Massachusetts

Historical Society in Nov., 1795, show that he was also interested in geology, mineralogy and archaeology. [4]

In order to help support the home, young Titus became a land-surveyor, no doubt under the tutorage of his father's next-door neighbor and old friend, Theophilus Chamberlain (1737-1824), who had become a deputy-surveyor of the province and a man of prominence generally. From then until shortly before Smith's death, a very large number of Crown Lands Office plans and descriptions bear his modestly written signature.

On 17th August, 1796, two months after the arrival of the Jamaica Maroons in Nova Scotia, the elder Smith sold, for £325, much of his Preston land (part of Lot No. 4, Letter A, and also Lot No. 2, Letter C, in all 230 acres), to W.D. Quarrell, their official agent;[5] and on 22 October following purchased for £80 from Martin Wagner a small house, farm and woodland of fifty acres, being Lot No. 1, originally granted in 1763 to Frederick Kohl, a German, at the northernmost end of Westerwald or 'Westervolt', also known

---

[4] A photostat copy of the elder Smith's letter which is preserved in the records of the Mass. Hist. Soc., is before me. It occupies four foolscap pages, is addressed to J. Clarke, and dated at Preston, 10 Nov., 1795. In it he treats at some length of his (Smith's) extraction of alum, Glauber's salt, and common salt from the mud of salt-marshes near New Haven, Conn., and at New York; of his discovery of calcareous 'asbestos' in a ridge of rock to the westward of West Haven, a parish of New Haven, Conn.; and in Nova Scotia of an earth answering the character of 'melinum'. With his letter he sent an Indian stone implement, like a large arrowhead but without a tang, found at Preston. He had shown it to and Indian who said that with smaller arrowheads they shot the moose, but that larger implements like the present one were never used but to kill men, and that they used them in their wars with one another. Smith goes on to say that 'as to vegetables, we have several here which I cannot find in Linneus; but samples of them cannot be taken till their season for blossoming returns next summer'.

[5] On 13 Dec., 1802, he also sold, for £40, to Charles Morris the 3rd, 80 acres of land on the west side of Lake Loon, near Preston. This formed part of Morris's country estate.

as the Dutch Village. The lot was bounded on the north by the present line of the main part of the old highway of about 1812, known as the Geizer Hill Road, one part of which was run through the east end of the Smith lot. His house, now gone, was among apple and other fruit trees, a few rods west of the junction of the Dutch Village and the curving part of the Geizer Hill Roads, not far from the house of the late Mr. Levi Deal. To this land he added in the same and following years, twenty-two and a half acres, mostly woodland, adjoining on the north, purchased from one Tracy Dennis. [6] Here the father and son continued farming, gardening, growing fruit and raising stock, while devoting their spare time to study and thought.

We now come to a notable period in the life of the younger Titus. He had become widely known as a young man of the most marked ability, which resulted in his being selected to carry out an important and arduous enterprise. On 2nd May, 1801, when in his thirty-third year, he and Mr. Carter were instructed by Lieut.-Governor Wentworth to make for the Government a careful survey of so much of Nova Scotia as could be accomplished within fifty days from the day he should set off, unless renewed (as it afterwards was) by special order. For this service he was to receive 11s. 8d. Halifax currency, each day for himself, and 8s. for Mr. Carter, during actual services, for pay and every contingency. Such was the value placed upon capable technical services in that period!

The full text of the Governor's instructions is given in Mrs. Lawson's 'History of Dartmouth,' page 209. It may be briefly stated that he was to visit the most unfrequented (interior) parts of the province, particularly the banks and borders of rivers, lakes and swamps, and the richest uplands, in order to discover the spots best suited for producing hemp and finishing other naval stores, such as pine for masts and

---

[6] It had originally been granted, I believe, to one Abraham.

juniper for ship's knees. He was to note the character of the soil, situation of the lands, and the species, quality and size of timber, and the quantity of each sort, as well as the facility with which it might be removed to market. The thickness and length of mast-timber was to be attended to in an especial matter. In every place which he should deem suitable, he was to estimate the number of acres, the possibility and means of rendering them fit to cultivation either by banks, drains or otherwise. He was to receive a map of the province and to correct errors on it. He was always to use the (place) names used by the present inhabitants, and to refer to a table of Indian and French names introduced of then late years into the maps of the province. To some extent he might investigate the objects of natural history, so long as this did not cause delay or draw him away from the main objects of his research.

As to the itinerary indicated to him, he was directed to proceed first to the *eastward of Halifax* to the headwaters of the Stewiacke, Musquodoboit and St. Mary Rivers, or wherever else the objects of his enquiry were to be found. Then he was to proceed to the *western section* of the province and to examine the lands about the St. Croix River and St. Margaret's Bay, after which he was to travel along the northern side of Chester, Lunenburg, Liverpool, Shelburne and Argyle as far as Yarmouth, and to the heads of those waters which empty into the Atlantic. The examination of the great Lake Rossignol was to be a principal object of this part of his tour. If necessary, the rivers which flow into Annapolis Basin and the Basin of Minas were to be examined; and possibly also the mountains south of the Annapolis River, paralleling the Bay of Fundy. The last region to be investigated was the *inland country* between Rhemsheg (Wallace) and Bay Verte in the northeast, and the Basin of Minas in the southwest. His journey must have taken him through some of the wildest parts of the counties of Halifax, Guysborough, Pictou, Colchester, Cumberland, Hants,

Lunenburg, Queens, Shelburne, Yarmouth, Annapolis and Kings.

I wonder if anyone at the present time would care to undertake such work at about $2.34 a day for pay and all expenses! But of course, money had more purchasing value then than now. The total expense of the survey was only £181.4.8 Halifax currency or about $724.90.

Smith immediately set forth and carried out his instructions in a thorough and highly satisfactory manner. His eastern tour occupied from 5 May to 19 June, 1801; the northern one from 1 Sept. to 16 Oct., 1802; and the examination of the lands between Sackville and Shubenacadie, 26 Oct., 1802. When the western tour was undertaken, I am not now sure. The arduous nature of his tour may be realized when it is known that it was practically always in the unsettled, densely forested, inland districts; for he only visited settlements in order to obtain a renewal of his supplies.

A transcript of the journal of his eastern and northern tour is preserved in the Public Records of Nova Scotia, vol. 380 (cap). It contains a vast amount of interesting original information, and has an appendix (pages 145-179) dealing with the trees and shrubs of the province, their habitat, characters, and the uses to which their timber could be put, and also a list of indigenous plants – this being the first such accurate list that had ever been compiled. [7] The original vellum-covered, well-filled note-book of his western tour, which book had been reported missing since 1838, was found by me among the books of the late Dr. T. B. Akins. All of these notes on his first-hand observations, bear evidence of the careful and thorough manner in which he carried out the task assigned him. If Smith had accomplished nothing more than this, it should make his name on to be always

---

[7] These lists of trees (27 pp.), shrubs (3 pp.), grasses (1 p.), and other plants (5 pp.) give both their common and scientific names.

remembered in this province. It is extremely probable that the military settlements made soon after 1814, were places in districts upon which he had favorably reported.

The revised map which he turned in with his report, was only reliable one of the province until July, 1834, when William Mackay prepared and published a new one under a special grant from the Legislature.

For some forty years after this, Smith continued to be employed in making ordinary land surveys in various parts of the province, and this gave him opportunities of increasing his already remarkably extensive and accurate knowledge of our natural history and varied resources, and he became an authority on our fish, the fisheries and the commerce connected therewith.

On 4 January, 1803, he married Sarah ('Sally') Wisdom, daughter of Henry and Lucy (Scott) Wisdom. [8] By this marriage he had a large family which will later be referred to.

His saintly father died on 15 Sept., 1807, at the age of seventy-three, and thereupon the well-kept Dutch Village farm, which they had together tilled for more than a decade, fell to the son who for so many years had loyally stood by and assisted his ageing parent. His step-mother, Lydia Smith, passed away in 1818.

---

[8] As to the date of Smith's marriage, it is stated in Mrs. Lawson's History of Dartmouth that he died on 4 Jan., 1850, 'on very anniversary of his marriage forty years before', which would make the year 1810. I have been unable to find a newspaper notice by which the date of the marriage might be verified. In a letter of 10 July, 1802, from Titus, Senr., to his son William, the former refers to Titus, Junr's, courtship with a young girl, but does not mention her name; and a descendant, Mrs. E. M. Cole, Newton Centre, Mass., gives the date of the marriage as 4 Jan., 1803, which is no doubt correct, as it agrees better with the above statement by the elder Smith.

In 1815 there had come to Halifax from Scotland, John Young (1773-1837), who three years later published in the 'Acadian Recorder,' under the pen-name of 'Agricola', a series of epoch-making articles on agriculture. In 1819 Young established himself as a model farm which he called 'Willow Park', which Smith passed on his way from and to the Dutch Village, and as the two had much in common in their deep interest in agriculture, horticulture and the improvement of live-stock, they soon became fast friends.

In that interesting and rare book, 'A General Description of Nova Scotia', published at Halifax in 1823 and again in 1825, and which I believe was mostly prepared by Walter Bromley, though some think it was by T. C. Haliburton, there appears on pages 34-38 of the 1825 edition, a long 'List of Plants indigenous to Nova Scotia', giving both the common and scientific names, which was prepared by Dr. C. R. Alderson of the 62nd Regiment, with, it states, 'the assistance of that valuable member of society, Mr. Titus Smith'.

When the Halifax Mechanics' Institute, which played a notable part in the education growth of the town, was organized in Dec., 1831, Smith naturally took a keen interest in its work, and from time to time delivered before its large and attentive audiences well-thought-out lectures on various subjects. One of there, a 'Lecture on Mineralogy', delivered on 5 March, 1834, was considered to be of such interest that it was published at Halifax in that year as a pamphlet of thirty-six pages. The next year there appeared in 'The Magazine of Natural History', edited by J. C. Loudon, London, vol. 8 (1835), pp. 641-662, an article by him entitled, 'Conclusions on the Results on the Vegetation of Nova Scotia, and on Vegetation in general, and on Man in general, of certain Natural and Artificial Causes deem to actuate and affect them'. It is of a general nature, giving some account of the soil, trees, ferns, fungi, etc., of Nova Scotia. A number of individual species are referred to, but no attempt is made to provide a systematic or exhaustive catalogue of them. It was more the relation to agriculture that the writer had in view, and he ends with a plan for the improvement and extension of agriculture in a world that is suffering from the over-production of manufactures. [9]

In the early 'thirties Smith published a notice that, as imported garden seeds were apt to fail, probably from the want of progressive naturalization, he had on hand homegrown seed of the most common vegetables, which he believed to be free from that defect. Having also given much time to the study of botany, he was prepared to furnish collections of the indigenous plants of Nova Scotia, and their seeds, to anyone who desired to avail themselves of his services. On this occasion our newspapers drew attention to Smith's outstanding attainment, but regretted that his unobtrusive merit had not been crowned with all the appreciation it deserved. (See Mullane, 'Footprints around Bedford Basin,' 1912, pp. 13-14.)

In 1832, under an Act of the Legislature, he had surveyed and marked the then newly constituted boundary between the town of Halifax and the rest of the county – a straight line from the head of the Northwest. Arm to the brook at Fairview, Bedford Basin – and set up three uninscribed granite monuments to establish that line. The last of these three-foot obelisks, the center one, was not removed until the Terminal Railway was constructed about 1914.

In the autumn of 1838 he was honoured through being selected by the Lieut.-Governor as one of those to represent Nova Scotia in giving evidence at Quebec before the Earl of

---

[9] This article in the 'Mag. Of Nat. Hist.' was reprinted at the suggestion of 'R.G.' (Dr. Robert Graham of Edinburgh?) and was a paper which Smith had read before the Halifax Mechanics' Institute on 14 Jan., 1835, and which had been printed in a Halifax newspaper under the heading, 'Natural History of Nova Scotia'.

Durham's general commission of enquiry for crown lands and emigration, which had been appointed on 21st June. The delegates went from Halifax to Quebec in H.M.S. 'Medea' which arrived there on 12th September. Smith's evidence (appearing by a misprint under the name Silas Smith) occupies some twelve foolscap pages (18-29) of the printed copy of the evidence which was published at Quebec in 1839. His statements show the wide extent and carefully considered nature of his first-hand knowledge of the entire province, of the quality of its land and its suitability for settlement and cultivation, its timber and other natural resources, information of which his survey of 1801-2 made him such a master as no one else could be. This trip to Quebec, is the only instance, so far as I know, of his having gone beyond the province since his arrival in 1783.

At this time there was rising into prominence a talented young Halifax artist, Miss Maria Morris, afterwards Mrs. G. T. N. Miller, (1813-75), who began to specialize in flower-painting in water-colours. About 1834 Smith began to collect for her, choice specimens of the common and rare wild flowers, which she portrayed in a superb manner; and below each painting he neatly printed the plant's common and scientific names. As the beautiful series rapidly grew, friends urged its publication, and in 1839 or 1840 the first part of the famous but never-completed serial, 'The Wild Flowers of Nova Scotia', began to be issued in London under the patronage of Lt.-Gov. Sir Colin Campbell, as quarto-size hand-coloured lithographs, with suitable descriptive text by Smith. Three of the lovely plates were to be in each part, the price of which was five shillings. After only two parts had appeared, the publication had to be suspended, owing to the great cost of production and the lack of enough subscribers in a sparsely settled colony. This deprived us of having in printed form a record of Smith's most finished botanical work.

It may be added that after Smith's death, two other equally unsuccessful attempts were made to continue the publication. In 1853 parts 3 and 4 appeared with text by the Rev. Alexander Forrester, D.D. (1805-69), under the patronage of Sir Gaspard Le Marchant; and in 1866 parts 5 and 6 were issued with text by Dr. George Lawson (1827-95), under the patronage of Sir W. Fenwick Williams of Kars; but each attempt also failed for lack of support. Had the project been fully carried out, we would have had such a series of coloured plates and descriptions of our beautiful wild flowers as has not been surpassed in any other country.

Ninety-nine sheets of Miss Morris's original paintings, 16 by 12 ins., representing 146 species, named by Smith, and painted about 1834-5, but not those used for the above-mentioned publication, became the property of the Halifax Mechanics' Institute and are now a priceless possession of the Provincial Museum of Nova Scotia, where they attest to her consummate skill in portraying the pose, colouring and texture of the flowers of our fields, roadsides and woods. The whereabouts of the artist's own set of paintings, is now unknown, although some years ago it belonged to her daughter, the late Mrs. James Alpine Grant of 34 Russell St., Halifax.

From time to time he contributed articles, probably all modestly unsigned, to such Halifax newspapers as 'The Nova Scotian' and 'The Acadian Recorder', on useful subjects of every kind, but more particularly on agriculture, rural economy, botany, geology, chemistry, history, and education in general.

At a meeting held at Halifax, 27 Sept., 1843, at which the sectarian college system was condemned, Joseph Howe delivered a ringing speech against such a system, in the course of which, in regard to the Acadia College professors of philosophy and divinity, he said: 'I would go down to the Square and take a man off of his market cart, who should teach these professors philosophy; and when I name Mr.

Titus Smith, is there a person in this audience who will dispute the fact? I think you will agree that not only could he teach them much of which they are ignorant and should be taught in a college, but that he has forgotten more than either of them ever learnt.'

For many years Smith was the efficient secretary of the old Central Board of Agriculture,[10] and during part of the period was the editor of an agricultural periodical. Also for some years before his death, he prepared for 'The Acadian Recorder', Halifax, a weekly article on agriculture, and at the time of his decease had several weeks' material ready for the printer.

In the autumn of 1849 he had an attack of jaundice which he tried to ward off by taking an unusual amount of exercise. For fear of alarming the members of his family, he told them nothing of his illness. Gradually he grew worse, and finally passed away, at the age of eighty-one years and four months, at his simple home at the Dutch Village, on Friday, 4th January, 1850, the very anniversary of his marriage forty-seven years before. The good, learned, venerable Dutch Village Philosopher had gone to his final rest. His passing was heard of with profound grief by the entire province in which he had been so well known and held in such high esteem.

The 'Acadian Recorder', Halifax, of 12th January contained an obituary notice, from which the following fine tribute is extracted: 'We think Mr. Smith was utterly incapable of provoking enmity in any human heart. Apparently he recognized no distinction in the rank of individuals, but such as vice or virtue makes-never changing his demeanor in addressing any person, whether exalted or humble, intelligent or ignorant. Though unaffected in his address, he was invariably affable and gentle towards all

---

[10] The Central Board of Agriculture appears first in Belcher's Almanac for 1842.

with whom he had any intercourse. Indeed, he was 'in wit a man, simplicity a child'. Had circumstances placed him in a different sphere, we believe he possessed one of those giant intellects which is the production of an age, and capacitates its possessor to figure prominently in the world's history. But his was a different lot, and if it was cast among the humble-if the influence he produced is destined in a great measure to be local-his memory is less likely to be defamed by those who attribute all deserved repute to the promptings of pride and selfish ambition. There are few of our citizens who were not familiar with the simple habits, the benevolent feature, and the venerable mien of this worthy and remarkable man.'

At his request he was buried in a small, private, unconsecrated burying-ground of his own, in which some of his children, his father and his step-mother, as well as some of the old German settlers were interred in graves merely marked by small, uninscribed slate boulders. This secluded cemetery was on a hillside overlooking the blue waters of Bedford Basin, in the midst of a growth of birch, pine and other trees, near the north end of Dutch Village Road and nearly half a mile west of Fairview. [11] It was just such a charming, peaceful, bird-frequented woodland spot as a retiring lover of nature and a thoughtful village philosopher would choose for his eternal sleep. Some years later (at least after 1866) his admirers erected on the spot a six-and-a-half-foot high, grey granite obelisk, on which were merely carved his name, the date of his death and his age.

The Nova Scotian Institute of Natural Science, on one of its earliest field-days, a very hot 26 June, 1866, made a

---

[11] It is about 240 yards northward of the bend of the Geizer Hill Road, 630 yards westward of Fairview, and 350 yards from the shore of Bedford Basin; and its elevation is 110 ft. The 20 ft.-square lot in which Smith is buried now belongs to his great-granddaughter, Mrs. H. D. Brunt of Macdonald College, St. Anne de Bellevue, Quebec. About two acres of the cemetery adjoining, has, I understand, been made over to the community.

pious pilgrimage to the grave, and gathering around the grass-grown mound, listened with reverently bared heads while their president, J. Matthew Jones, read an account of his long, useful life. At the close of these proceedings, anecdotes and reminiscences of the departed worthy were related by many who had known him and admired his rare talents and markedly unobtrusive virtues. (See 'Proc. And Trans. N. S. Ins. Nat. Sc.', vol. 1, pt. 4, pp. 149-152.) In the many years since then, the place has become neglected and overgrown by brambles and weeds, and houses have arisen close to it; but from time to time one of the younger generation chances upon the lichen-covered obelisk and wonders who was this Titus Smith, whose name he had never even heard!

He had a large family, some of whom died young, others of whom went away in order to make a living. [12] At least four daughters married in Nova Scotia and have left descendants. Olive L. (born 1811, died 14 April, 1893, aged 82) married John P. C. Bayer, (1811-90), of Halifax, son of George Philip Bayer and grandson of George Bayer a prosperous German settler from Frankfort-on-the-Main. They were the parents of the late Rufus O. Bayer, a gentleman who inherited much of his maternal grandfather's fine qualities and quiet disposition. Charlotte married Donald Grant, son of James Grant, of East Gore, Hants Co.; Harriet Sophia (1827-85) married in 1848 the late William A. Hendry (1823-1908), of the Crown Lands Office, Halifax; and Rebekah married a Mr. Parker, of Walton, N.S. I have often talked about Smith with two of these sons-in-law.

---

[12] Mr. C.J. Creighton of Halifax, who married a daughter of W. A. Hendry, has recently compiled the following list of Smith's family, which, however, may not be in chronological order, as the family-record of the naturalist is not available: Titus; Mary Ann; Charlotte, m. Donald Grant; Olive L., m. John P.C. Bayer; Harriet, died young; William; Henry; Sarah; Harriet Sophia, m. W.A. Hendry; John; Rebekah, m. a Mr. Parker of Walton, N.S.; Eliza; and Emily. He apparently left no sons in Nova Scotia.

As to his appearance, we have only to guide us a small three-quarter-length oil portrait, copied by a very mediocre artist, Karl Jensen, from a now-lost original sketch by Mrs. Miller (*nee* Maria Morris), which original I have never seen but which is said to have been lent to the late J. J. Stewart who died at Halifax in 1907. [This portrait is alarmingly bad. The proportions are wrong, making Titus look like an alien. Craig Balzer tamed that portrait while preserving the overall appearance - WCR] I think that this portrait must have been painted not long before his death, or at least after 1843. It represents him as very venerable man, rather pale-looking, deeply wrinkled, thin-faced but rosy-cheeked, clean shaven, but with a noticeable shock of long white hair which hangs down in locks on his forehead and in large curls to his shoulder, but with scanty eyebrows, and light-blue eyes. He is clad in loosely-fitting black garments, wears a white bow-tie, and in his hand are gold-rimmed spectacles. He stooped a good deal, which made him appear short, but his son-in-law said that at the time of his death they were surprised to find that he measured nearly six feet. [13]

Despite his slight build, he had an unusually hardy constitution, a result of his habitual outdoor life. He was never heard to complain of fatigue or seen to lie down during the day. His work as a surveyor often led him into marshy land, and it is said that whenever he got a pair of new boots he immediately bored gimlet-holes in the soles, so as to let out the water which would necessarily get in.

In religion he, like his father, the Howes, Chamberlains, Greenwoods, Stayners, Allens, Fosters, Dechezeaus, Crowes, some of the Lawsons, Pierses, and other prominent families of the Loyalist period, was an adherent of the now almost extinct Sandemanian (Glasite) Church, which, with other doctrinal tenets, held scrupulously to the most literal interpretation of the Bible, the very

---

[13] His brother, Sylvester, was also about six feet tall.

strictest probity of conduct, a certain amount of community of good and of interests, a bounded duty to assist their fellows and a very sincere humility of disposition. There was no paid clergy, their elders supporting themselves solely through their ordinary occupations. The most notable member of this somewhat primitive but truly virtuous sect, was the great English scientist, Michael Faraday (1791-1867).

As one result of his religious views, Smith believed in the fundamental equality of man, and therefore thought little of high birth of honorary titles; and so was equally at ease in the presence of persons of stations as in that of the most humble labourer. He only esteemed men for their goodness and knowledge. He was always a poor man, for he set little value on wealth, requiring only what was needed to supply the ordinary wants of his simple, everyday life; and so was liberal in unostentatiously giving to others what he himself did not absolutely require. This necessarily entailed considerable sacrifice on the part of his family.

Naturally he was a man of unfeigned simplicity, modesty, gentleness and kindness, which, with his store of helpful knowledge, made him a welcome visitor wherever he went. In demeanour he was noticeably quiet, humble, and retiring. His temperament was a most equable one, he being rarely much elated or depressed; and he was never known to have been angry. His brother wrote that he thought it might with literal truth be said of Titus, that from two years of age he was never known to cry and seldom to laugh; yet he was youthful and cheerful up to the last.

His memory was remarkable, He would recite long portions of Hesiod's 'Work and Days', often repeat a whole chapter of the Bible, or give an entire scene from one of Shakespeare's plays, a poet whose works he is said to have read at one sitting when his father got them after they went to Preston. In speaking on an historical subject he talked as if reading from a book. In conversation his sentences were long; but in writing he used short, concise phrases.

As a striking illustration of how absorbed he and another notable man could become in a subject, I have often heard my father, whose family knew him well, tell how on one summer evening Smith and John Young ('Agricola') became deeply engrossed in a discussion about agriculture. As a chilly east wind was blowing, the two enthusiasts sat in the convenient shelter of a stone-wall just opposite to our old home at Willow Park, and there, oblivious of everything else, they talked on and on, until one of them happened to notice a peculiar glow in the eastern sky. To their dismay they found that they had talked through the entire night!

We must now discuss his accomplishments, and first will consider his standing as one of the pioneer naturalists in this province. He was the first (if we except the lesser, amateur or dilettante work of his father) who seriously took up the study of systematic botany as known after the appearance of the epochal work of Linnaeus; for the old travelers had merely noted what plants they had met, usually under the common names of similar, but not the same, plants in Europe. We may take it that Smith's serious botanical investigations, on a modern basis, began in 1790 or '91, when his father was presented with the botanical works of Linnaeus; and that date, I think, marks the commencement of scientific taxonomical botany in Nova Scotia. His specific identifications still hold good, considering the changes in nomenclature which have since taken place. Wherever he went, he diligently searched for plants, examined and classified them, observed their habitats and characters, and learnt their uses, all of which he recorded. He also introduced some rare or interesting indigenous plants and shrubs into his own and some of his friend's gardens. As an example of this, about 1822 he planted a large variety of fine trees in the grounds about my grandfather's house in the northwest suburbs of the town, and introduced into the garden there, such rare wild species as the Red Baneberry (*Actaea rubra*), the frail white Bloodroot (*Sanguinaria canadenis*), and the aromatic American Spikenard (*Aralia racemosa*). The Bloodroot was thriving when we left the place in 1897, and the Spikenard, after having been transplanted to Armdale, still flourishes after the passage of about a hundred and fourteen years.

As we might except, he possessed dependable knowledge of the medicinal properties of our wild and cultivated plants, and was frequently called in to prescribe simple and reliable countryside remedies for many of the common ailments of those about him. Numbers of persons used to testify to the cures he had thus effected.

He corresponded with such eminent men as Francois Andre Michaux (1770-1855) of Paris, botanist and traveler, author of 'North American Sylva' (3 vols., 1810-13); with that prolific Scottish writer on horticulture and agriculture, John C. Loudon (1783-1843); and with Dr. Robert Graham (1786-1845), professor of botany at Edinburgh; Dr. Grey of the same place; as well as with others in Europe and America; and some of these incorporated in their writings information from this region supplied by the Nova Scotian botanist. We have already referred to his account of the trees, shrubs and plants appended to the report on his survey of 1801; to the assistance given Alderson in the preparation of a long list of our native plants in the 'General Description of Nova Scotia', 1823 and 1825; and to his work in connection with Miss Morris's 'Wild Flowers of Nova Scotia', 1839-40.

Taking all this into consideration, I think it may quite justly be claimed that he was the first scientific botanist to study and to make known directly, or too often indirectly through others, the flora of this region; work which was later continued by such men as Drs. Alderson and William Cochrane (1757-1833, who came to Nova Scotia in 1788), and still later ones such as Drs. Lawson (1827-95), How (1828-79), Somers (1840-98), MacKay (1848-1929), and Lindsay, (1853-1915).

Besides his major accomplishments in botany, he made observations to determine the names, characters and habits of our mammals, birds and fishes, although, so far as I know, not directly publishing anything on the subject: and as has been said he was a decided authority on the fishing industry. Lists of our fauna appeared in the 'General Description of Nova Scotia', 1823 and 1825, in Haliburton's 'Nova Scotia', 1829, and in Dawson's 'Handbook of the Geography and Natural History of Nova Scotia', 1848, but I am not in a position to say if Smith assisted in the compilation of any of those lists, although we might suppose that in some cases he had. In the study of our birds he was followed much more thoroughly and successfully by the Rev. Dr. Thomas McCulloch (1776-1849), who had arrived at Pictou in 1803 and later began to collect and study birds, of which he gathered a fine collection which Audubon examined in 1833. He was followed by Andrew Downs (1811-92) in about 1832. Although the 'General Description of Nova Scotia', 1823, Haliburton, 1829, and Dawson, 1848, gave partial lists of our fishes, with their common and scientific names, it was not till the appearance of Perley's (1804-62) 'Catalogue of the Fishes of New Brunswick and Nova Scotia' in 1851, that those animals became really well known.

To the study of geology, then somewhat in its infancy, and mineralogy, he devoted considerable attention, and as we have seen he lectured on the subject in 1834. It is difficult to say how far he may have antedated Jackson and Alger (1827) and Gesner (1836) in this field, but he could not but have been a close and enquiring observer long before they worked here, for an intelligent agriculturist had to study the soil, and the rock from which it was derived.

In local history he was one of our very best-informed men, for from the time of his arrival he had taken pains to increase his knowledge by obtaining directly from the early settlers - French, English and German - authentic stories and traditions, which he critically examined; and these were freely imparted to interested students, and some were published anonymously in the Halifax newspapers. He has thus been the means of preserving remarkable details of some otherwise little-known persons, things and happenings; such as accounts of the original government house of 1749; of the old maple-tree which was used as a gibbet; Robert Cowie and his unfortunate servant who was unjustly hanged for the supposed theft of a silver spoon; four men who were executed because it was thought they intended to steal; the drunken old public hangman, 'Tomahawk', and his woeful end; the old Naval Hospital, its architect, Brooks, and his utterly debauched son, and that building's destruction by fire. These interesting traditions appeared in 'The Nova Scotian' for 29 Dec., 1842, page 410. Other articles dealt with such subjects as the supposed treasure on Oak Island, an account of a deserter from H.M.S. 'Jason' who blew up the American privateer 'Young Teazer', etc. [14] Many other such stories by him are no doubt hidden away in the columns of our local newspapers, those little-explored storehouses for such things. It is much to be regretted that a worthy proposal made in 1850 to collect and publish his writings was never carried out. Most, however, of his wide knowledge on various subjects passed with him at his death.

To sum up: if we date, as I believe we may, his intensive systematic studies of nature as having begun about 1791 (at the age of 23), we may claim that he was the first man, so far as we know, who scientifically, studied our plants, mammals, birds and fishes – that is, our first true naturalist since the Linnaean period. With the probable exception of the Rev. Dr. Andrew Brown, who was in Halifax from 1785 to '95, and whose extensive material for a history of Nova Scotia is in the British Museum, he was the first to make a study of our history. He and his father were probably our first scientific and experimental agriculturists and

---

[14] I think these traditions were published in 'The Acadian Recorder' or 'Nova Scotian' soon after Smith's death. Unfortunately, I cannot find the transcripts of them which I made.

horticulturists; being followed in agriculture by John Young (1773-1837) in 1815, and in horticulture by Hon. Charles Ramage Prescott (1772-1859) of Cornwallis after about 1812, the latter being the first to promote and improve fruit-growing in that section of the province.

The principal reason why Smith's store of knowledge has not been perpetuated in readily accessible printed form, is that there did not then exist in Nova Scotia special publications, such as we have had since 1862 in the Transactions of the N.S. Historical Society, in which he could publish the results of his investigations; and independent publication in book or even pamphlet – form was entirely beyond his meagre resources, as well as repugnant to his modest nature. His unsigned occasional contributions to our newspapers are buried among columns of news and the prolific writings of a period of political agitation covering a long period. In his time, however, through his lectures, his conversations, and his correspondence, he was able to do much to inspire thought and increase knowledge in a young colony in which the study of philosophy, science and history was in a backward state. He was always ready to furnish others who had better opportunities for publication, with the results of his pains-taking information on to those who were interested, but not in the full manner in which he himself could have done it.

Such is a brief account of the life and accomplishments of good old Titus Smith, the Dutch Village Philosopher, one of the most able and at the same time one of the most modest men Nova Scotia has ever had.

Authorities Consulted.

1795. *Smith (Titus), senr.* Letter regarding occurrence of Alum, Glauber's Salt and Calcareous Asbestos, in Connecticut, etc., and of Melinum and an Indian Stone

Implement in Nova Scotia. Dated, Preston, 10 Nov., 1795. Mass. Historical Soc., Boston.

1801-2. *Smith (Titus), junr.* Survey of the Eastern and Northern Parts of the Province, in the years 1801 & 1802, with General Observations thereon; also a Survey of Lands between Sackville (Bedford) and Shubenacadie, and Observations on the Western Parts of the Province; with a List of Trees, Shrubs, Grasses and Plants, and Observations on the Nature and Uses of the Trees. Transcribed 1857. Public Records of N. S. vol. 380, 179 pp. Contents: Eastern Tour, p. 1; Northern Tour, p. 43; General observations on Northern Tour, p. 118; Lands between Sackville and Shubenacadie, p. 122; General Observations on Western Tour, p. 125; List of Trees, p. 145; Shrubs, p.171; Grasses, p.174; and Plants, 175-179.

1825. *Bromley (Walter), or Haliburton (T. C.).* General Description of Nova Scotia. Anon. Halifax, 1825 (1st. ed. 1823). Dr. Alderson's and T. Smith's list of plants of Nova Scotia, pp. 34-8.

1834. *Smith (Titus).* Conclusions on the Results on the Vegetation of Nova Scotia, and on Vegetation in General, and on Man in General, of certain Natural and Artificial Causes deemed to actuate and affect them. Read before the Halifax Mechanics' Inst., 14 Jan., 1835. Mag. Of Nat. Hist. (J. C. Loudon ed.), London, vol. 8, 1835, pp. 641-62.

1839. Minutes of Evidence taken under the direction of a General Commission of Enquiry for Crown Lands and Emigration, appointed 21 June, 1838, by His Excellency the Rt. Hon. The Earl of Durham, High Commissioner and Governor General of H. M. Colonies in North America. Quebec, 1839, foolscap size. Pp. 18-29 contains the evidence given by 'Silas' (*sic*) Smith who had arrived in Nova Scotia in 1783.

1839 or 40. *Morris (Miss Maria)*, and *Smith (Titus).* Wild Flowers of Nova Scotia. Coloured plates after Miss Morris's paintings; text by Smith. Halifax and London, 1839 or 40; quarto size; only 2 parts (of 3 plates each) issued

1842. *Nova Scotian* (newspaper). Halifax, 29 Dec., 1842, p. 410. Anonymous historical notes by Smith.

1847. *Sabine (Lawrence)*. American Loyalists. Bost., 1847, p. 621. Short sketch of T. Smith, senr.

1850. *Acadian Recorder* (newspaper). Halifax, 12. Jan., 1850. Obituary notice of Smith (partly quoted in Lawson, 1893, p. 218, footnote)/

1863. *Boltwood (L. M.)*. Family Genealogies; appended to Judd (S.), History of Hadley Mass. Northampton, Mass, 1863, p. 571/ Genealogy of the Smith family to which Titus belonged; and the source of information on the subject.

1866. *Nova Scotian Institute of Natural Science*. Proc. And Trans. Halifax, 1866, vol. 1, pt. 4, pp. 149-52. Account of pilgrimage to Smith's grave on 26 June, 1866, with address on his life by the President, J. Matthew Jones, and a long and important letter, dated Mar., 1850. Dealing with the life of the Smiths, father and son, written by our Titus Smith's younger brother, William Smith (1771-1858) of Watertown, N. Y.

1867. *Murdoch (Beamish)*. History of Nova Scotia. Halifax, 1867, vol. 3, p. 220. Appreciative remarks on Smith and his work; quoted in Lawson, 1893, pp. 213-4.

1867. *Morgan (Henry J.)*. Bibliotheca Canadensis. Ottawa, 1867, o. 352. Short article on Smith.

1891. *Archibald (Sir Adams)*. Deportation of Negroes, Coll. N. S. Hist. Soc., vol. 7, Halifax, 1891, p. 139. An extract from Lt. John Clarkson's Journal of 1791, referring to Smith's father.

1893. *Lawson (Mrs. William)*. History of Dartmouth, Preston and Lawrence-town. Halifax, 1893, pp. 205-218. Sketch of life of Smith by his son-in-law, Wm. A. Hendry; one of the main sources of information about the naturalist.

1896. *Dexter (Prof. Franklin Bowditch)*. Biographical Sketches of Graduates of Yale College, with Annals of the College History, vol. 2, New York, 1896. Sketch of Rec. Titus Smith, senr. The main source of information about him.

1909. *Howe (Hon. Joseph)*. Speeches and Public Letters. Ed. by J. A. Chisholm. Halifax, 1909, vol. 1, p. 431. Howe's laudatory reference to Smith in a speech of Sept., 1843.
1912. *Mullane (George)*. Footprints around and about Bedford Basin. Halifax, (1912), pp. 13-4.
1915. *Piers (Harry)*. Brief Historical Account of N. S. Institute of Science. Proc. N. S. Inst. Sc., Halifax, vol. 13, 1915, pp. liii-lv.
Also verbal information from *William A. Hendry* (1823-1908), Smith's son-in-law; *Henry Piers* (1824-1910), who knew Smith; *Rufus O. Bayer* (1841-1926), Smith's grandson; *Mrs. Thomas Ibson* (b. 1850), grand-daughter of Smith's younger brother, Sylvester; all of Halifax; and *Mrs. E. M. Cole*, Newton Centre, Mass, one of Smith's descendants. Also various old letters to members of the Smith family, belonging to Titus's granddaughter, *Mrs. Chas. J. Creighton* (nee Hendry).

INSTRUCTIONS

May 1801

To Mr. Titus Smith Jr.

Sir:

Government having expressed a desire that means should be adopted in this province to encourage the growth of hemp, at the recommendation of a committee appointed for that purpose, I have thought it proper to accept your offer, jointly with Mr. Carter, to make a survey of so much of the peninsula of Nova Scotia, as can be accomplished within the periods herein limited; and you will take the following instructions as your guide.

1st. You will consider your engagement to expire at the end of fifty days reckoning from the day at which you shall set off, unless renewed by an express order, in writing from myself or the secretary of the province; for which service you shall receive eleven shillings and eight pence, Halifax currency, each day for yourself, and eight shillings each day for Mr. Carter, during your actual service; in full for your pay and every contingency. You will contrive to be so situated on or a little before the fiftieth day, as to hear from me, or the secretary of the province.

2nd. Your principal object in this survey will be to visit the most unfrequented parts, particularly the banks and the borders of the different rivers, lakes and swamps, and the richest uplands, for the purpose of discovering such spots as are best calculated for producing hemp, and furnishing other Naval Stores. You will make your remarks on the soil, the situation of the lands, and the species, quality and size of the timber, the quantity of each sort also, and the facility with which it can be removed to market. The thickness and length of mast timber, you will attend to in an especial manner, and in every place which you shall deem calculated for these purposes, you will as near as possible estimate the quantity of acres, the possibility and means of rendering them fit for cultivation either by banks, drains or otherwise.

3rd. You will receive from the Surveyor General such a map of the province, as our present knowledge of the country can furnish: you will endeavour as far as lays in your power to correct any errors in it, and on your return you will deliver me the same, with another containing these corrections, and the route which you shall have gone distinctly placed on it.

4th. You will in the first instance go to the eastward of this harbour, to the spot from whence issue the heads of the River's Stewiacke, Musquodoboit and Saint Mary, and wherever else in consequence of the information you may receive, you may be led to suppose the objects of your enquiries are to be found. Having examined the eastern side of the province, from the Shubenacadie, the Dartmouth Lakes, and the Harbour of Halifax, you will proceed to the western side and examine the lands about the River St. Croix, and the land of St. Margaret's Bay and thence along the northern side of Chester, Lunenburg; Liverpool, Shelbourne and Argyle, as far as Yarmouth, and the heads of those waters which empty themselves into the Atlantic. You will endeavour to examine Lake Rossignol, and will consider it to be a very principal object of your tour. You will trace those rivers as far as anything desirable is to be obtained from such an investigation towards their mouths, which empty themselves into the river Annapolis or the Basin of Minas; and if within your power, without losing much time, you will examine the mountains which run parallel to the Bay of Fundy, to the southward of the Annapolis River. The last object of your researches will be the inland country situated between Bram shag and Bay Verte in the NE and the basin of Minas in the SW.

5th. What is expressed in the second and fourth article of these instructions you will consider as your principal objects;

but if in the course of your travels, you should meet with any other subjects in Natural History, or find any inducements of importance the investigation of which is evidently for the benefit of the public, you will use your discretion, provided they do not occasion any essential delay, or in any respect draw you away from the main object of your research which must not on any account, be sacrificed or even impeded.

6th. You will not omit to give me any information in your power by the fourth day of June next, after which you will forward your intelligence by every favourable opportunity. In order to facilitate the present design, I have given directions to the Secretary of the Province to deliver you a circular letter directed to all the magistrates and other persons throughout the province to afford you all the assistance in their power, but you will take care not to require anything from them which shall occasion an additional expense to the Government.

7th. Your communications will be in the form of a Journal with reference to notes at the end, which will contain the detail. You will always make use of the names used by the present inhabitants, and refer to a table of Indian and French names and terms with a view of correcting the arbitrary names of late years introduced in the maps of this province.

J. Wentworth, Lieut Gov.

Halifax, Nova Scotia May 2nd, 1801

LIST OF TREES & PLANTS			
Common Name	Genus	Species	Note
Larch, Hachmetac or Juniper	Pinus	larix	
White Pine	Pinus	strobus	
Yellow Pine	Pinus	silvestria	
Hemlock	Pinus		
Balsam Fir	Pinus	balsamifera	
White Spruce	Pinus		
Red Spruce	Pinus		
Black Spruce	Pinus		
Mountain Pine	Pinus	pinea	
Black or Yellow Birch	Bitula	nigra	
White Birch	Bitula	alba	
Dwarf Birch	Bitula	nand	
Beech	Fagus	silvatica	
Sugar, Rock, Curled or Birdseye Maple	Acer	saccharinum	
Red, Flowering or White Maple	Acer	rubrum	
Moosewood Maple	Acer		
Dwarf Maple	Acer	mana	
Elm	Ulmus	americana	
Hornbeam	Carpinus	ostria	
Pigeon Cherry	Prunus		Black Cherry

LIST OF TREES & PLANTS			
Common Name	Genus	Species	Note
Red Cherry	Prunus	avisim	
Choak Cherry	Prunus	virginica	
White Cedar	Thuya	occidentala	
Trembling Poplar	Populus	trembla	
White Poplar	Populus	alba	
Mountain Ash or Fowler's Service	Sorbus	aucuparia	
Wild or Indian Pear	Mespilus		
Oak	Quercus	rubra	
White Ash	Fraxinus	americana	
Black Ash	Fraxinus		
Shrub Maple	Acer		
Alder	Bitula	alnus	
Balsam Poplar	Populus	balsamifera	
Buttonwood or Sycamore	Platanus	occidentalis	
Lime Tree	Tilia		
Thorn	Crataegus	crus galli	
Fox Berry	Melpilus	canadensis	
SHRUBS			
Witch Hazel	Hammamelis	virginiana	this always flowers in autumn, usually in October
Pond Bush	Cephelanthus	occidentalia	

LIST OF TREES & PLANTS			
Common Name	Genus	Species	Note
Water Elder	Viburnum	opulus	
Withrod	Viburnum		
Moose Bush	Viburnum	lantania	
Maple Leaved Viburnum	Viburnum	acerifolium	
Red Berried Elder	Sambucus	racemosa	
Black Berried Elder	Sambucus	nigra	
Black Currant	Ribes	nigrum	
Red Currant	Ribes		
Catnip Scented Red Currant	Ribes		
Gooseberry	Ribes	uva crispa	
Red Willow	Cornus		
Pigeon Berry	Cornus	canadensis	An herb-aceous plant
Red Berried Honeysuckle	Lonicera	alpigena	
Blue Berried Honeysuckle	Lonicera	xylosteum	
Oicivilla	Lonicera	dierilla	
Thorn Apple Bush	Prinos		
Evergreen Gall Berry	Prinos	glaber	
Winter Berry	Prinos		
Black Whortle	Vaccinium	myrtillus	
Swamp Whortle	Vaccinium	frondosum	

LIST OF TREES & PLANTS			
Common Name	Genus	Species	Note
Red Whortle	Vaccinium	vitis idaea	
Blue Berry	Vaccinium	album	
Crane Berry	Vaccinium	oxycocos	
Maidenhair	Vaccinium	hispidulum	
Labrador or Indian Tea	Ledum		
Crimson flowering bush	Rhododen-dron		
Wild Rosemary	Andromeda	frolifolia	
Round-leaved Andromeda	Andromeda	calyculata	
Raspberry	Rubus	idaeus	
Blackberry	Rubus	fructicocus	
Dewberry	Rubus	saxatillis	
Creeping Blackberry	Rubus	hispidus	
Bog Apple	Rubus	chamamorus	
Dalibarda	Rubus	dalibada	
Spiraea Frutex Red	Spiraea	tomentosa	
Spiraea Frutex White	Spiraea	salcifolia	
Candleberry Myrtle	Myrica	cerifera	
Dutch Myrtle	Myrica	gale	
Sweet Fern	Myrica	asplini folio	
Juniper	Juniperus	communus	
Savin	Juniperus	sabina	
Dwarf Laurel	Kalmia	augustifolia	

LIST OF TREES & PLANTS			
Common Name	Genus	Species	Note
Willow, 3 species	Salix		
Silver-leaved Laurel	Kalmia	glauca	
Berry-bear	Empetrum		
Bear Berry	Arbutus	uva ursa	
Poison Ivy	Rhus	radicans	
Sumach	Rhus	canadensis	
Ground Hemlock or Dwarf Yew	Taxus		
GRASSES			
Seeded Swamp Grass	Briza	media	
Blue Joint Grass	Agrostis		
Tickle Grass	Agrostis		
Blue Swamp Grass	Agrostis		
2 other unknown species	Agrostis		
Wild Millett	Panicum	breve folium	
Small Wild Oat	Avena	spicata	
Maiden Cane	Arundo		
Elymars	Elymus	canadensis	
Elymars	Elymus	arenarius	
Aria, 2 species	Aira		

LIST OF TREES & PLANTS			
Common Name	Genus	Species	Note
Bearded Thatch Grass	Dactylis	aynosurrides	
Cotton Grass	Eriophorum	alpinum	
Sedge Grass several species	Carex		
Rushes (3 species)	Juncus		
Sweet Flag	Acorus	calamus	
Blue Flag	Iris		
Chair makers flag	Typha	augustifolia	
PLANTS			
Enchanter's Nightshade	Circosa	alpina	
Bladderwort	Utricularia	subulata	
Blue-flowered Grass	Sixyrinchium		
Twinberry	Mitchella	repens	
Blue Solomon's Seal	Convallarua	polygonatum	
Solomon's Seal	Convallarua	racemosa	
Tongue	Convallarua	trefolia	
Indian Cucumber	Convallarua		

LIST OF TREES & PLANTS			
Common Name	Genus	Species	Note
Single-leaved Lily-of-the-Valley	Convallarua	bifolia	This plant does not flower until it is several years old. Until it does flower it has but one leaf and afterwards assumes two.
3 nondescript species of Convallaria	Convallarua		
Houstonia	Houstonia		
Broad-leaved Plantain	Plantago	major	
Sea Plantain	Plantago	maritima	
Shepherd's Needle	Scandix	fracten	(pevten)
Sweet Cicely	Scandix	adorata	
Sarsparilla	Aralis	nudicaulis	
Prickly Sarsparilla	Aralis	spinosa	
MEDICINAL PLANTS			
Spikenard	Aralia	racemosa	
Hairy Plantaun	Plantago	lagopus	
Convolvulous	Convolvulous	avensis	

LIST OF TREES & PLANTS			
Common Name	Genus	Species	Note
Cow Parsnip	Heraculum		
Seashore Loveage	Ligusticum	scoticum	
Ground Nut	Claytonia	virginiana	
Ground Nut	Burrium	bulbocastenum	
Canada True Love	Trillium	erectum	
Nodding Trillium	Trillium	corimum	
Bog Beans	Menyanthus		
Sea Cabbage	Cyncoglosum		
Dogbane	Apocynum		
Asclepais (12 species)	Asclepias		
Statice	Statica	limonium	
Blue-flowered Pond Weed	Pontidera	cordata	
Chickweed Wintergreen	Trientalis	europaea	
True Primrose	Oenothera	biennis	
	Oenothera	perennis	
	Oenothera	parviflora	
French Wikkow	Epilobium	augustifolium	
	Epilobium	polustre	
American Sanicle	Mitella		
Princes Promy	Pyrola	umbellata	
Wintergreen	Pyrola	rotundifolia	

LIST OF TREES & PLANTS			
Common Name	Genus	Species	Note
	Pyrola	secunda	
Mountain Tea	Gaultheria	repens	
Bear Berry	Arbutus	uva ursi	
Mayflower	Ehigola		
	Arenaria	2 or 3 species	
	Lythrum		
Cohosh	Actoea		
Indian Cups	Sarracena	purpurea	
Chocolate Root	Geum		
	Geum	Montanum	
Goldthread or Snake Root	Heleborus	trifolius	
Wild Tulip	Tulipa	sylvestris	
Herb Robert	Genanium	robertianum	
	Genanium		
Dragon Root	Arum	triphyllum	
Bloodroot	Sanguinaria		
Fumitory	Fumaria	cuculata	
Fumitory	Fumaria	spectabilis	
Fumitory	Fumaria		
	Baccharia		
	Cardemine	trifolia	
	Leontice	thalictroides	
	Caltha		
Yellow Violet	Viola	canadensis	
Blue Violet	Viola	palustris	
Cancer Root	Luthaea	clandestina	
Linnea	Linnea	corealis	
	Chelone	acadiensis	

LIST OF TREES & PLANTS			
Common Name	Genus	Species	Note
	Thalictrum	disecum	
St. John's Wort	Hypericum	canadensis	
	Hypericum		
	Saggitaria	saggitifolia	
Thistle	Cardirus		
Mullein	Verbuscum	phlomoides	
Royal Rocket	Verbuscum	phoenicum	
Green Briar	Simula	rotundifolia	
	Souttilaria	laterifolia	
Kali	Salsola	kali	
	Hanthium		
Dock	Rumex	patientia	
Dock	Rumex	persicaroides	
Dock	Rumex	matitimus	
Thoroughwort	Euparirium	perfolialum	
	Euparirium	purpureum	
	Lobelia	dortmannas	
	Lobelia	inflata	
Orchis - many nondescript species	Orchis		
Orphris - many nondescript species	Orphris		
	Orphris		
Ladies Slipper	Cypripedium		
	Poligala		
	Senicio	aurens	
	Senicio		

LIST OF TREES & PLANTS			
Common Name	Genus	Species	Note
Hawkweed	Hieracium	3 species	
Goldenrod	Silidago	several species	
Milkweed	Sonchus	carulius	
	Lapsana		
Autumnal Dandelion	Leontodon	autumnal	
Aster - several nondescript species	Aster		
	Aster	cordatus	
Virgins Bower	Clematis	vitalia	
White Water Lily	Nymphea	alba	
Yellow do	Nymphea	bitra	
Wood Sorrel	Oxalis	acetosella	
Wood Sorrel	Oxalis	corniculata	
Everlasting	Gnaphalium	uligoneum	
	Gnaphalium	margaritecum	
	Gnaphalium		
Five Finger	Potentilla	reptens	
Goose Grass	Potentilla	anserina	
	Potentilla	tridentata	
	Potentilla	fruticosa	
	Potentilla	nowgica	
Strawberry	Fragaria		
	Polygonum	parsicaria	
Arse Smart	Polygonum	hydropiper	
	Polygonum	lagittatum	
	Polygonum	convolvulus	

Originally published in Halifax Monthly Magazine, I (1830 – 31): 342-45. The preceding table is adapted from the typed transcript in the provincial Archives.

LARCH, HACKMATAG, OR JUNIPER

This is the strongest and most durable timber among all the trees of the Pine kind, which we have, but it does not grow to a large size being seldom more than a foot diameter. It is seldom used for any purposes, except making fencing poles, for which it answers better than any other timber, but the poles should not be too small, for the sap which is usually about an inch thick, decays very soon. It grows naturally in very barren places, either upon very poor, dry, gravel, upon rocks, or in cold mossy swamps.

WHITE PINE

This tree is the tallest of any that grow in our woods, although it does not come near the height of White Pine of New Hampshire and some other parts of the American states: here we consider it to be a large pine, which is 3 feet diameter, and 60 feet high to the branches. I have seen a few trees which were 4 feet diameter. The timber is generally more shaky (full of small cracks) than it is in the States: owing probably to the high winds which bend the trees backwards and forwards, and to the situation of the trees which most commonly grow by the sides of lakes, where they are much exposed to the winds.

The use of this tree is well known, oars are chiefly made from it as are also shingles, building timber, masts, yards; etc. There is no timber we have so easily worked.

It grows naturally in every kind of barren soil whether wet or dry. It is to be found in all rocky barrens, but it is there so short and scrubbed as to be of no value. The best pine are to be found on a sandy soil, which is not very rocky or very near the sides of lakes.

YELLOW PINE

This is frequently called Pitch Pine, but I do not think there is any real pitch pine in the province. This is a better tree for mast timber than the white pine of this country when large enough as it is usually straight which is seldom the case with white pine and it has no branches till near the top. A tree 2 feet diameter is generally 60 feet high to the branches. It grows in the same soil as white pine but is much more scarce.

HEMLOCK

This is one of our largest trees: it is commonly from 2 to 3 feet diameter, and 60 or 70 feet high. It has the figure of the White Pine as the trunk diminishes very little till it reaches the branches which usually begin about 40 feet from the ground. This tree is remarkably shaky which prevents it from being much used for plank or boards, or even for building timber. It is used for wharf logs and all our laths are made from it. The most valuable part of it is the bark which is very good for tanning leather. The blood is used for fuel by the bakers but it crackles too much to burn in an open fire. It grows most commonly on gravelly soils, which are poor, but better than the soil of pines. It grows also, but more rarely upon a clayey soil, which is sometimes very good.

BALSAM FIR

This is not a large tree, being seldom more than 15 inches diameter. It is very straight and tall, and forms a very regular cone by means of its branches. The wood decays very soon if exposed to the weather. It is much used to make small tubs and buckets as it is very light. It is also much used for fencing poles and pickets, as it is more frequently found of a proper size for these uses than any other kind of wood. The balsam is contained in thin white membranaceous bladders which lie in the substance of the bark very near the outside. It abounds most in those trees which are thrifty and grow the fastest provided they are shaded. That balsam is best which is collected from the tops of very young trees, being much more valuable and pungent than that which is found upon old ones. It is a good remedy for pains in the breast, internal bruises, and the rheumatism which is the consequence of hard drinking.

The bark of very young trees is mucilaginous: a decoction of this is often useful in the gravel and in most cases where directions are needed. It is of great use in long continued coughs, which threaten a consumption and may be given in safety where the balsam itself cannot on account of fever. The balsam is applied to fresh wounds, but it frequently does harm causing inflammation. The Indians make a kind of poultice of it by scraping and beating the bark of very young trees into a mucilage which is a very good application to fresh wounds: fir grows in almost every kind of soil, but thrives best in that which is moist and rich.

WHITE SPRUCE

This is a large tree, much resembling the red spruce: it is however a hardwood and a stronger timber. It is never used for making small beer as it has a disagreeable smell and taste. It grows on poor gravelly land, and is not plenty in any place that I have seen.

RED SPRUCE

This is the tallest tree we have except the white pine. It is commonly straight. The top takes the figure of a cone. It is much used for building timber, mast timber, and boards, and sometimes for shingles: it is stronger than white pine but the boards are much inferior to Pine for many purposes, as they decay much sooner if exposed to the weather, are very hard to plane, and very subject to warp and shrink. It is more plenty than pine, and consequently more used for mast and building timber. It grows in dry gravelly land in general which is neither very fertile nor very barren.

BLACK SPRUCE

This is probably a variety of the red spruce, occasioned by the difference of the soil. It grows in the most barren places, on rocks, in wet mossy swamps, and on very barren land or gravel. The wood is harder than that of Red Spruce, owing to its slow growth for every kind of softwood is hardest in the part where the grains or years growth join and consequently the timber is firmest in those trees which grow the slowest as this hard part is of nearly the same thickness, whether the grain is thick or thin. The leaves are a trifle larger than those of Red Spruce and have a little difference in their taste.

The use of this for making beer is well known. The Red Spruce is sometimes also used in beer but is said to give it a purgative quality. I imagine that this is owing to turpentine, which is much more commonly sticking to the branches of the Red than the Black Spruce. The black spruce when large enough the timber is much inferior to the red for the grain always twists very much, and it is almost always very knotty, the branches growing nearly the whole length of the tree.

MOUNTAIN PINE

I have never seen this tree, except on the tops of high hills of rock where it is necessarily very short and scrubbed, so that I cannot judge what size it might grow to in suitable soil. It is very scarce, its leaves are not more than half the length of those of White Pine. The cones (strobile) which contain the seed, differ remarkably from those of other pines being nearly as hard as bone.

BLACK OR YELLOW BIRCH

This differs a little from the Black Birch of New York being a stronger kind of timber, and the bark of the young seedling trees being always yellow here whilst at New York it is black. This difference may be occasioned by the difference of climate as ours agrees with the black birch of Linnaeus. This is a large tree frequently 3 feet diameter. The bark sometimes used for tanning leather, but is not accounted equal for this purpose to that of Hemlock. It is much used for ship building, both for timber and plank, and it is said to be less liable to damage from worms than oak, on account of the bitter gum which it contains. It is also much used by cabinet makers for household furniture. Bedsteads said to be made from the heart of birch are said to be free from bugs. The hoops used by the coopers at Halifax are made from yellow birch, as are all cart wheels. This tree is almost always to be found on good land and often on a very poor soil. It enriches the land where it grows. If the soil be poor it frequently sends out horizontal roots to the distance of 50 or 60 feet.

WHITE BIRCH

This tree always forms the principal part of such forests as grow up where the original growth of timber has been destroyed by fire provided the soil is not extremely barren. The outer bark is an article of great consequence to the Indians if it contains a kind of rosin which renders it almost incorruptible in the weather and impenetrable to water. Their canoes are made by covering a slight frame of thin laths with the bark. They choose for this purpose, that which is sound and near 1/8 of an inch thick. They then sew the different pieces together, with the roots of spruce or larch split in halves and cover the seams with spruce rosin. These canoes are lighter than could be made from any other materials and are easily carried from one lake to another. The Indians also frequently cover their camps with this bark and some few have tents made of it, by sewing a number of pieces together which they carry with them in their canoes. They always have at their camps a clumsy vessel made of birch bark to fetch water in with it also they very neatly make bowls to put their soup in, baskets and boxes ornamented with the quills of the porcupine dyed of various colors--As it burns with a fierce flame they use it for flambeaus to spear salmon, eels, lobsters, and other fish which they catch by night--The wood itself is the worst fuel we have, and is not much used for any other purpose except charcoal for which it answers very well.

DWARF BIRCH

This is only a small shrub. It grows on mossy bogs.

BEECH

This forms the greater part of the woods in our best land, what is called hardwood land being generally chiefly covered with beech, with a small proportion of birch and maple. It forms our principal fuel. Our new cleared land fences are commonly made from the logs, but they soon decay: if they are split into rails, they will continue good for three times as long as whole logs. Sleds are commonly made of this wood, and it is sometimes used for barrel staves, but it is not, as yet, much worked for any other purpose. Hogs are fattened with the nuts in those seasons in which they are plenty: but as far as I have observed they are blasted about half the year.

SUGAR OR ROCK MAPLE

This tree when it has its full growth is from 2 to 3 feet diameter. It abounds principally in the eastern parts of the province. The land is always very good where this tree is frequent. It grows chiefly in moist ground, near small brooks and upon intervals. This is very frequent upon limestone land.

The sap or juice which yields the sugar will run from the trees if cut or wounded in any warm day after middle of December. It will run at that season very slowly and continues to increase in quantity till the middle of April which is about the time that it ceases to flow when the weather becomes so warm as to swell the buds of the trees, and loosen the bark. The season for making sugar is commonly between the middle of March and the middle of April. The sap runs only in warm days which are preceded by a frosty night. If the weather should continue warm, the sap will seldom run for more than 24 hours, it then stops, and does not run again till there comes another frosty night. The sap is best in the beginning of the season: it then yields the most and the best sugar. The very last sap is commonly fit only to make molasses. At the beginning of the season 4 gallons wine measure will yield a pound of sugar. At the close it will require 5 or 6 for the same quantity. Such trees as are left in cleared land will yield more sugar from the same quantity of sap, but they do not produce as much sap as those which stand in the woods. There is no kind of work which requires a more constant attention than making maple sugar, as the running of the sap depends so much on the changes of the weather. For this reason, the greater part of those who attempt to make it do not manufacture the third part which they might with a little care and attention. The trees ought to be tapped with a chisel or an augur as they will then continue good for a long time, but when tapped with an axe as is commonly the case they are much sooner exhausted. It is a good season in which the trees yield two pounds of sugar each on average.

The wood of this tree is very hard and solid, it is superior for fuel to beech or birch--it is very frequently curled the grain running in small waves, and sometimes but more rarely, becomes what is called Birds' eyed by having the substance of the wood full of very small knots. Trees which are curled near the ground, are often birds' eyed above. The curled or birds' eyed maple makes very handsome furniture--Hard maple is frequently used for felloes for cart wheels, but it decays very soon when exposed to the weather.

RED, FLOWERING, WHITE, SOFT MAPLE

This tree grows upon almost every kind of soil. It thrives most near the water. It is covered with red flowers very early in the spring before the leaves appear, and the leaves generally change to red on the approach of autumn. It is harder than the soft maple at New York, but it is much inferior to it for timber as the grain twists very much. It is sometimes used by chair makers to turn; but they commonly prefer yellow birch. It makes good fuel, when dry, but very indifferent when green.

MOOSE-WOOD MAPLE

This is a small tree, very rarely more than 4 inches diameter; it is not used for any other purposes, that I know of except for fencing stakes: it is of a very quick growth and the wood is very soft and brittle. Its twigs are the principal winter food of the moose where they can find it (for it does not often grown on very barren land). It is in most plenty near small brooks, in stony hemlock land.

DWARF MAPLE

This is not above half the size of the last mentioned species. It is a very troublesome bush upon new cleared land, as it grows very fast, is not easily destroyed.

ELM

This tree is very rare, except on the intervals in the eastern part of the province: there it grows to a large size, often 3 or 4 feet diameter. It is a firm solid kind of wood, the bark is very tough and strong and is used to make ropes and chair bottoms. The ashes of any given quantity of elm will yield more potash than the ashes of four times as much beech or birch.

HORN-BEAM

This tree grows only upon good land especially intervals. It is seldom of a large size, it is the hardest and strongest wood we have: it is much heavier than water, and will sink in a swift stream. It is the best timber for axe-helves, rake teeth, etc.

BLACK OR PIGEON CHERRY

This tree is very rare except upon intervals; it is not so large in this province as in the United States further southward where it is often used to make tables, as it has nearly the color of mahogany. In Nova Scotia it is seldom more than 16 inches diameter. The fruit is small growing in long bunches. It is when fully ripe pretty good to eat, and is accounted very good to put into spirits.

RED CHERRY

This tree is seldom more than 16 inches big. It commonly springs up on dry stony land after a fire. The fruit is small and very sour.

CHOAK CHERRY

This is only a bush, being seldom more than 2 inches big. It is common upon interval by the sides of brooks on rich moist upland. It has long branches of fruit rather larger than that of either of the other two species, but is scarcely eatable, having a disagreeable astringent taste.

WHITE CEDAR

This tree grows in no place that I know of except in the valley of Annapolis River, and there it is not plenty. It is not the same tree which is called White Cedar in the southern States, although there is no great difference in the timber. It is excellent for shingles, tubs, and buckets, being very durable and not so apt to imbibe water as white pine. The same quality makes it good for building ships or boats, but it is so scarce in this province as to be of no consequence.

TREMBLING AND WHITE POPLAR

These trees differ but little from each other, they always grow upon land that has been burnt over, along with the white birch. They are tall but seldom more than 16 inches diameter. The wood is soft and light and is used to make trays. It is sometimes sawed into boards, it is springy and very bad to saw, it makes but poor fuel for common use, yet it is very good for charcoal.

MOUNTAIN ASH OR
FOWLERS SERVICE

This is a small tree, very rarely 6 inches diameter, it grows most frequently on very poor land. The bark of this has very nearly the same taste as that of the cherry tree. It is the favorite food of the beaver, and I believe it is the natural breeding place of the insects which destroy so many apple trees near Halifax by covering the branches with small nests which resemble lice, having frequently observed the bark of this tree covered by them, in places which were 20 miles from any settlement.

WILD OR INDIAN PEAR

This is a species of Medlar (Mespilus). It seldom exceeds 6 inches diameter. It grows most commonly on barren land, near to water, it is a remarkable flowering tree, and bears very good fruit about the size of cherries. It is, however, very frequently blasted. The wood is very hard and smooth and is sometimes used for axe helves.

OAK

We have but one species of this tree, that I have seen: it resembles the Red Oak in the States, but is harder and stronger. It grows chiefly on poor land, the best I have seen was upon very sandy intervals. It is more durable when exposed to the weather than any other kind of hardwood we have. It is used for plank and timber for ships, for staves for fish barrels, cartwheels, and many other purposes. It is scattered over every part of the province, but that which is of such a size as to be valuable is mostly in the eastern district.

WHITE ASH

This is a very tall tree, and a very strong and useful kind of wood (except when it grows in cold swamps where it is soft and brittle). It usually grows on rich land, and by the sides of brooks. It is very light and easy to split. It is the most suitable timber to make handles for tools, ploughs, carriage wheels, and for many other purposes. When green it is better fuel than any other wood we have.

BLACK ASH

This grows only in swamps, which, though rich, are sometimes so wet as to require draining to produce grass. The Canada flour barrels are made from this tree, but I have never seen any great quantity of it, of a size fit for staves in this province. It is here used to make baskets: to fit it for this purpose it is beaten with a maul which separates the grains or years growth. It makes very bad fuel when green.

SURVEY OF THE EASTERN AND NORTHERN PARTS OF THE PROVINCE

IN THE YEARS 1801 & 1802

WITH GENERAL OBSERVATIONS THEREON

ALSO, A SURVEY

OF THE LANDS BETWEEN

SACKVILLE (BEDFORD) AND SHUBENACADIE

AND OBSERVATION ON THE

WESTERN PARTS OF THE PROVINCE

WITH A LIST OF TREES, SHRUBS, GRASSES,

AND PLANTS

AND OBSERVATIONS ON THE NATURE AND

USES OF THE TREES

BY TITUS SMITH JR

HALIFAX

1857

3d Edition

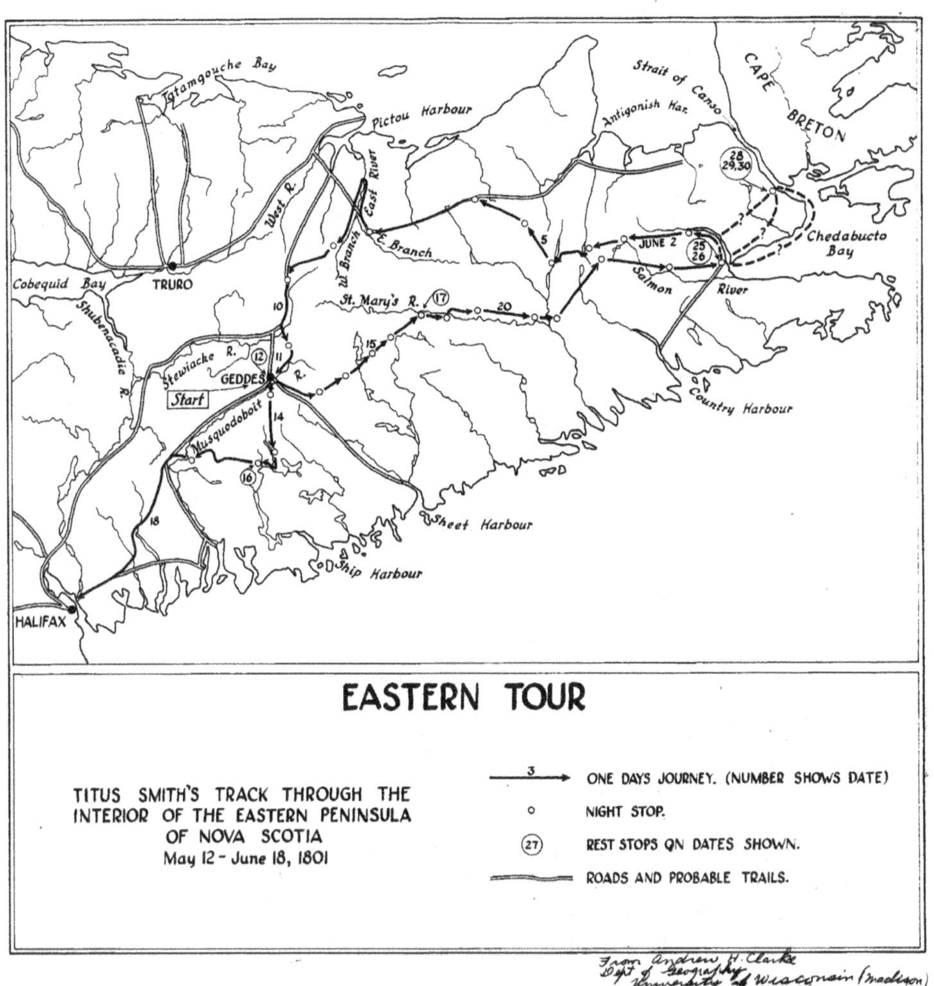

35 Days
267 miles

<u>May 5, 1801</u>

We left Halifax and reached Geddess where we resolved to enter the woods, some part of this time we were detained by bad weather, and by making such inquiries as might be useful to us. From the information we received from Col. Robert Archibald, we had reason to conclude that the head or upper settlement of Musqueduboit lay 8 or 10 miles nearer to the sea coast than it is laid down in our map: and we were informed by others, who had traversed that part of the country, that the land to the westward of the road from Geddess to Sheet Harbour was chiefly barrens, with not more good land anywhere in once piece than 100 or 200 acres. We therefore concluded to shape our course accordingly.

We learnt from different persons who had made small experiments on this river that hemp succeeded well on it. The intervals everywhere have so much of very fine sand in them as prevents clods and I think hemp would succeed well on them.

Part of the upland which has limestone on it is undoubtedly well calculated for the same purpose, but the greater part of the upland is too wet and clayey.

Col. Archibald showed us a kind of red Ochre with which he has painted his house, of which there are large beds in his neighbourhood. It is of a brighter color than common Ochre. He informed us that in the river near his house there were beds of pipe clay, and that there was plenty of mountain iron-ore higher up, near the Souiac. We were also informed that there was plenty of Plaister of Paris about three miles above Geddess, and that coal had been seen by persons going through the woods from Geddes to Souiac.

As we had reason from the information received to expect that we should be obliged to traverse very rough ground we concluded we should not be able to carry provisions to last us any length of time; we therefore, resolved to go a suitable distance into the woods and then steer so as to strike Saint Mary's River 10 miles above the fork: then to follow the river to the fork, and (if we could there supply ourselves with provisions from the settlers, or should find game sufficient to support us) to trace the north branch as far as it should appear worth following and afterwards to steer for Pictou.

12th We started from Geddess Mill and proceeded 8 miles S. 65 East, we then changed our course to N. 64 E. and went 1 mile, when we pitched our camp. At the end of 6 miles we touched the N. E. corner of a lake about a mile across a small brook runs S. from it.

The land this day about half hardwood and half spruce barrens. Seldom more than 200 acres of hardwood in a piece. After we were 1 ½ miles from Geddess Mill, the land, both good and bad, nearly level, no hill of more than 10 or 12 feet declinity in a ½ of a mile. The barrens though almost wholly beds of stone, show scarce any as they are covered with turf. At the end of 8 miles we touched the N. end of a large, nearly level burned barren, which extended from 6 to 8 miles to the S. E. and round to the S. beyond which we could see hills of hardwood and hemlock.

We passed the northern extremity of it where it was about 3/ [?] of a mile broad.

We had this day passed two pieces of barrens which were covered only with moss without bushes.

13th Proceeded No. 65 E. 6 miles, at the end of 3 miles we passed a brook about one rod broad and 18 inches deep, where the current was strong and about a quarter of a mile farther another of the same size, their course S.E. At the end of 6 miles passed another of the same size, and within ten rods a fourth not much broader, but five feet deep, although the currant was very strong these two run S. and meet in a little lake just below. At the end of 4 miles we crossed a hardwood hill, about ½ a mile broad and 1 ½ miles long.

The rest of the land this day chiefly thickets of black spruce. The land continued level to the first brook we crossed this day. The stone from Musquedeboit River to that brook the blue mountain stone which is common about Halifax, from thence it changed to the coarse pebbly granite, and the land became very hilly and rocky.

14th Proceeded 7 miles in the same course. The first mile on hardwood which extended a mile to the left and farther to the right where we could not see the bounds of it.

As the thickets in the woods prevented our seeing any considerable distance, it was my practice to climb tall trees in favourable situations, to get a distant prospect. The next 5 miles we travelled on barrens very thickly covered with small black spruce, then one mile on hardwood. The land very hilly and rocky except a little hardwood, which however has a very gravelly soil. At the end of one mile passed a brook about the size of Tremain's mill brook (feet). At the end of 3 passed another, not quite so large, and a ¼ of a mile farther another about 2/3 the size of Salmon River at the new bridge. The course of all to the S.E.

15th Proceeded 5 miles the same course and were obliged to halt by the rain. Passed a brook the size of Tremain's (feet) at the end of a mile and a half.

At the end of 3 miles another of the same size. Course of both S.E. At the end of 4 miles touched the N. end of a narrow lake, which has a brook the size of the others, that empties into the W. end of it.

We could see the lake a mile to the south when it turned out of sight. The land this day chiefly hardwood everywhere hilly, and the half of it (all that has a mixture of soft wood) very rocky. Some of the hardwood has a very good soil.

16th Rained all day, but as we could procure no game where we lay, were obliged to proceed. Continued our course 10 miles to St. Mary's River. At the end of one mile passed a brook large enough for a mill. Half a mile farther touched a lake, which lay at our right for two miles. At the end of 5 miles passed a large brook running N.W. The land 1/3 hardwood of a good quality – 1/3 mixed hard and soft wood and very rocky; the remainder barrens. The hills very high, the good land is near their tops; the valleys are either beds of rocks or mossy spruce swamps. The stone is the coarse granite.

17th A steady rain, which detained us all day.

18th Went 5 or 6 miles down the river, our course very little S. of E. We spent a great part of the day in fruitless attempts to ford it in places where it divided into a number of streams, as it was so rapid and crooked, that we could not safely cross it on a raft. – For about ½ a mile in length, the interval is ½ a mile broad the rest 30 rods broad on an average it is low and often exposed to freshets, but very fertile. The timber is chiefly elm and pigeon cherry with an underwood of choak cherry, black elder, water elder, wild currants, etc. The blue joint grass is now one foot high and very luxuriant -- We also passed about 150 acres which lay 3 feet higher, but are not so fertile, it has been flooded to the height of 4 feet, 10 or 12 years ago. S of the river, there is good land for 1 ½ miles back, as far as I could see. On the N side I could not see above ¾ of a mile chiefly barrens.

<u>19th</u> Spent half the day in making a raft and crossing the river, went 6 miles down, its course E. 10 N. For a mile and a half 20 rods interval, then 2 miles none of any value. The remaining 2 ½ miles about 30 rods wide, a hardwood hill everywhere on the S side of the river, in some places separated from it by half a mile of spruce. On the N side burnt barrens, except a mile and a half of hardwood. In some places we could see hardwood about a mile and a half to the N.

<u>20th</u> Proceeded 10 miles down; the course E 15 S -- about 40 rods breadth of interval for a mile and a half then for 4 miles not more than 20 rods and higher than the other, but of a poorer soil. The remainder 40 rods breadth, very good within 4 miles of where we halted. We passed two pieces of interval containing each 40 or 50 acres in a square form. The greater part of what we had passed before was in small pieces, owing to the river running quartering across it from one bank to the other; for the last 5 miles the interval is so high as not to be exposed to common freshets, and is very heavy timbered with sugar-maple, beech, yellow-birch, and some elm. This would undoubtedly answer well for hemp or grain. The land on the North bank is chiefly soft wood; on the S almost everywhere hardwood.

<u>21st</u> Proceeded down the river two miles, the course E 20 S to the entrance of where the other branch which was nearly equal in size to the S branch. We could however see that there was more of a freshet in it than in the other. Being disappointed in our expectations of finding settlers from whom we might have received supplies and meeting with no game, as the rising of the water prevented our catching trout and there were almost no partridges on the river, probably owing to it having been so much hunted by Indians formerly, as we saw a multitude of their old winter camps, and had not the luck to see a bear: though several times we came to

where they had been 5 minutes before: we resolved to go to Country Harbour, for we had not above 2 days provisions.

As it was impossible to pass the N. branch of the river here, we proceeded up, but found ourselves hemmed in by two lakes and a large marsh in which we waded in about a foot of water for half a mile and were then obliged to turn back and take a circuit of 4 miles which brought us to the river according to our judgment, about 2 miles from its mouth that is the junction with the other branch. We followed 2 miles to the northwards where we forded it with some difficulty in a place where it was divided into 5 or 6 streams then proceeded S. 65 E. -- upon land chiefly hardwood with very little stone, from where we set off this morning to the fork the interval is near a mile broad on an average; heavy timbered with abundance of sugar maple. The soil is suitable for hemp or grain, although not secure against very great freshets. The N. branch has a march of 500 acres and two lakes which extend 2 miles to the northward end westward. The marsh is good for wild grass. The lakes appear by the number of Indian summer camps*about them to be much resorted to by salmon. Above the lakes for 2 miles there is interval from ½ to ¾ of a mile of a mile broad, very low and often flooded. The timber of a large size chiefly sugar maple, elm, yellow birch, and some oak. From the kind of plants which grow here, I should think this the most fertile spot we have passed. The S. side of the S. branch of St. Mary's appears as far S. as we could see, that is about ¾ of a mile, to be wholly hardwood, and in going up the N. branch and round the lakes we saw scarce any upland but hardwood.

22nd Proceeded N. 70 W. 4 miles when we found 7 or 8 small narrow lakes in our way. N. and S. the longest about a mile, between hills running the same way with small brooks, from them running S. the lakes continued about 3 miles, and we

---

* In Nova Scotia each Wigwam is called a camp.

were obliged to set off about ¾ of a mile to the N. to shun them. We then steered N. 65 E. for 9 miles when we pitched our camp.

The only brook of any considerable size we passed this day being rather larger than Tremain's, was 10 or 11 miles from St. Mary's running N. which we supposed to belong to Antigonish. All the other brooks we passed were very small and run S.

The land this day, the best body of upland we passed since we left Halifax. The soil is a mixture of loam and gravel, no rocks, the stones small, and not so numerous anywhere as considerably to impede the plough. The first 7 miles the land rather more than half hardwood, the remainder, lakes, firs, thickets and swamps. The swamps mossy and poor, the last 9 miles [??] of the land hardwood and most of the swamps of such a quality that with a little draining, they would make excellent grassland. We observed on some of the hardwood hills plants which usually grow only on intervals.

23rd As we found we had missed the head of Country Harbour, and that we always erred the same way, we concluded the points of the compass on our map were the true points of the compass, for we had followed the compass without making any allowance for variation. We now resolved to strike Manchester and continued our course N. 65 E. for one mile, then turned S. 75E. and went 7 miles where as we supposed it the river was about 2 rods broad and ran S. We passed it and changed our course S. E. to avoid land which looked like swamps and lakes; we followed the course for 6 miles and struck the river again, which here received a branch from the N. nearly equal to the other. The land this day for the first 8 miles nearly the same quality as yesterday, except that several places were very stony, the stone chiefly of the kind of which the black lime is made at Halifax.

The last 6 miles half swamps and thickets of fir. The swamps are all of a good kind, the upland inferior to what we passed before, the beech not so large and a considerable mixture of fir with it, the land not so stony as what we passed in the morning. The stone, part limestone, part a reddish kind, composed of a variety of pebbles cemented together.

24th Left the river and steered east about 10 miles when we struck Manchester church. The land growing gradually worse for 7 miles, as much as half thickets and swamps, two black spruce barrens about ½ a mile broad, but considerable pieces of a good quality for grass. The dry hills covered with small beech and a mixture of fir, the land stony.

We then went for a mile and a half on hilly land which by the timber on it appeared to be fertile although it was nothing but heaps of rocks, which were partly limestone, partly a kind of reddish freestone, the last mile and a half chiefly barrens composed of the same kind of freestone, some of which seems good for hewing, if it can be found in large pieces, for on the surface it is small, apparently broken by the fires; it is to be found composed of pebbles as large as peas and varying to a grain so fine that it can be scarcely be distinguished.

Both our course and distance, hitherto must be considered as very inaccurate for we have had very bad cloudy weather. As much as 8 days out of 12 that we have been in the woods have been cloudy or rainy. We have been for several days, obliged to travel when it rained the whole time, and we are much more liable to turn out of our course then when we have the sun to guide us; we have travelled many miles in black spruce thickets, where we were obliged to squeeze our way through the bushes, which were so thick, that we could seldom see two rods ahead, and when set the compass we could do little more than turn our faces the right way, and were then obliged to go constantly on a zig-zag line to avoid such places as were absolutely impassable. In some places we have been obliged to cross burnt barrens where the original growth of spruce had fallen within 3 feet of the ground, crossing each other every way, and a thick growth of young bushes had sprung up. In such places we could form but an indifferent judgment of the distance we travelled as we probably walked more than two miles to advance one. This may account for the shortness of some of our days' journies, which might surprise persons acquainted with our woods; but we never had more fatiguing days' journies than those in which we travelled the least distances.

As we cannot here get the articles we need of without considerable delay, particularly biscuit, and we are informed by people from the Gut of Canseau, that we cannot supply ourselves there, we intend if the weather is good to go there tomorrow and as soon as we can get ready to steer for the great lake at the Head of Antigonish, and from thence to the N. branch of St. Mary's which we shall trace as far as it appears of consequence, and then go to Pictou, from whence we shall probably return to Halifax as we judge by that time we shall need clothing and other articles, which we shall find it difficult to procure in this country.

I have forgot to observe that we have nowhere seen any quantity of timber suitable for masts or large spars.

<u>MANCHESTER</u>

25th Spent the day in writing.

26th Detained by bad weather.

27th Came to the Gut of Canseau, as there was no biscuit to be procured in Manchester, and we had been informed that we could supply ourselves with that, and other articles which we needed, at the Gut. We continued here 'till the 31st

employed in procuring necessaries and mending our clothes and other things.

The land near Manchester, and all round Chedebucto Bay, is of a broken kind. There are large tracts of hardwood land of a pretty good quality, and an equal quantity, I should think, of rough rocky ground, part of which the limestone land is fertile and may make tolerable pastures. The remainder is barren and of no use except for the small quantity of timber it produced.

There are a number of fine farms along the sides of the Milford Haven which show great marks of industry. The interval upon the brook which runs in at the head of Milford Haven is settled for about 4 miles above the salt water. It produces very fine crops of English hay which I was assured by some of the inhabitants suffered nothing from the uncommon drought las summer, but they complain of having their Indian Corn and potatoes frequently cut off by frosts in the month of August. I have observed that this interval lies between two very high hills of good land the tops of which I think from all I ever observed, as well as from information received in this town, would be perfectly secure against such early frosts, and out to be chosen for such things as are in danger of being ruined by them.

Along the Gut of Canseau there is a hardwood hill most of the way adjoining the salt water; it has a stiff loamy soil, and is very stony in some places. We were informed it produces remarkable crops of potatoes but there are no great improvements here, as the inhabitants spend great part of their time fishing. The hardwood seldom extends more than ¾ of a mile back from the salt water. Back of this place as far as we examined it, that is about 4 or 5 miles, the land is nearly level, and contains some barrens, covered with small black spruce, and a considerable quantity of swamp, mostly fit for draining but the greater part is covered with fir about 6 or 8 inches diameter. The soil is a reddish loam, with a mixture of very fine sand, very free from stones. We were informed that this kind of land has sometimes, when new and in good order, produced better crops than the hardwood; but it loses its strength much sooner than the latter, unless it is manured. The land about this place seems to be more productive than a soil apparently of the same kind near Halifax; which may be partly owing to the depth of the loose soil, which shows itself on the brooks here, as they have usually steep banks from 10 to 30 feet high. The stones here are likewise free from the sulphureous iron pyrites, so common in the slate near Halifax as to impregnate great part of the land with vitriol.

31st Left the Gut of Canseau and steered for Milford Haven.

1st Came to the interval; as the weather was bad, did not proceed into the woods.

June 2nd Left the interval about 4 miles N. of the head of Milford Haven and travelled W. 10 miles. The land 4/5 hardwood. For the first 7 miles it is very free from stone, what few there are, are small. The last 3 miles very stony; as much as 1/3 of it fit only for pasture. Some small pieces more fertile than any we passed in the morning. Stones almost all limestone. Spruce and pine very scarce this day not sufficient for building. Plenty of fir about one foot diameter. Pass no large brook. The small brooks have high banks, in general, and run mostly to the S. For 2 miles in the morning we constantly went up hill after which the land was always hilly, but the hills were neither very high nor very steep.

June 3rd Proceeded W. for 7 miles when we struck a lake about 2 miles long a little below the middle of it. We went to the head of the lake when we encamped, after spending some time in a fruitless attempt to pass a boggy marsh which extends some way to the southward above the lake. The lake runs, for above half the length from the head, a course a little W. of N. it then for the remainder bends to the N. E. The stream appears to run nearly N. where the stream runs into the head of the lake, it is not larger than Tremain's Mill stream (feet). Along the shores of this lake we saw considerable quantities of black sand which is wholly attracted by the magnet. The land for 4 miles 2/3 hardwood, but very rocky, mostly unfit for plowing, and several barren black spruce swamps. The stones chiefly of a reddish chocolate color, composed of pebbles cemented together. The last 3 miles the land hardwood and very fertile. The swamps chiefly good, the stone limestone in large rocks 1/3 of the land too strong for plowing. About a mile before we came to the lake we saw a limestone rock rising 30 or 40 feet above the top of the hill on which it stands; from the top of it we could see 10 miles to the E. the N.E. and N.W. it appeared to be all hardwood, but as the land was hilly there may be considerable quantities of soft wood in the valleys.

4th From the foot of this rock to the lake the ground falls as we judged not less than 150 yards perpendicular descent; this steep side hill is nevertheless extremely fertile. Passed the brook about ¾ of a mile above the lake and steered N. of W. till we judged we were again in our course and one mile W. of the lake, we then continued our course and one mile W. of the lake, we struck a lake on the head of the eastern branch of S. Mary's near its middle. It is as we judged, about 3 miles long although we could not see the head, but it turned so narrow that we thought it near. We followed the lake down to the S. and passed the brook which is here but little larger than Tremain's Mill brook (feet). For half a mile, as far as we followed it down, the interval is near half a mile broad, but low fit only for grass we then turned N.W. half a mile.

The land this day all hardwood, except about half a mile of barren thicket, and several small swamps which are very good being full of luxuriant chocolate root, but almost impassable owing to the alders being bent down by the snow in the last winter, none of the land very stony. The land for one mile E. of St. Mary's

[A page appears to be missing, although the sequence on the handwritten copy (20, 21) is correct]

and about a dozen broken salmon spears stuck in the bank, saw Gaspereaus in St. Mary's. This day we passed some brooks with steep banks more than 20 feet high although they were so small that we could easily step over them.

5th Went due No. 8 miles; halted before night on account of rain. The land for 4 miles very indifferent; rather more than half soft wood, very barren and rocky but has a considerable quantity of good building timber on it, the hardwood poor. The last 4 miles all hardwood, chiefly good although the soil is gravelly, and rather more dry than is usual for hardwood; it would probably suit well for winter grain. The gravel is chiefly composed of broken limestone. At the end of 5 miles passed a brook large enough for a mill, its course N.E.

6th Changed our course to N.W. and went 8 miles, the first 3 miles very good hardwood land, and then touched the N. end of lake about ¾ of a mile long, the brook running northerly, then for one mile barren rocky swamps and thickets containing some good building timber. The remainder nearly all hardwood and very fertile, but the last 2 miles so full of stones chiefly limestone that not more than one half of it can be ploughed. At the end of 5 miles we touched the N. end of a small lake, the brook from which runs southward. It is about the size of the trout brook in Preston (feet).

7th Continued N.W. for ¾ of a mile, and struck Blanchard's road from Antigonish to Pictou, in which we proceeded 18 miles westward to the E. branch of the N. river of Pictou and about 5 miles above the fork. The land for 5 or 6 miles all hardwood and very fertile but so full of limestone, that it would be difficult to plough the greater part of it. The remainder about half hardwood, with considerable tracts of barren land among it.

The greatest part of the hardwood is very strong, but many places very good for grass. Towards Pictou the limestone diminishes as the land grows worse, the stones there chiefly the coarse millstone granite. Within 2 miles after we struck the road we passed on stream running N., which we were told empties into Marigamishe. We afterwards passed several others which all run southwards toward St. Mary's. We were informed at Pictou that there is a large tract of barren land S. and S.E. of this place, and that there is abundance of Plaister of Paris a few miles above.

8th After supplying ourselves with provisions we left the W. branch of the East River about 5 miles above the Fork, and travelled W. 3 miles. We saw a considerable quantity of freestone between the two branches of this river, but all that lay above the ground was too much cracked and shivered to be of any use.

9th Proceeded W. 20 S. for 3 miles, then turned W. and travelled 6 miles, when we struck a path from the head of the middle river of Pictou to the head of Souiac, as the land grew worse we did not think it worth while to proceed farther westwards. We then followed the roads about 2 miles to the S.W. The land for 7 or 8 miles from the river is chiefly hardwood and pretty free from stone. The soil is a loam with a mixture of gravel, from thence to the path the land grows worse, some of the hardwood part spruce and hemlock, also a great quantity of fine spruce for building timber. There are some few spars 30 inches diameter at the butt; which may run 70 feet. Many about 20 inches and tall enough. The most barren part of this land is not very stony but seems to be sand on a bed of clay. Half a mile before we struck the path, we passed a brook running S. after following the path for 2 miles we passed another running E. where we lay.

10th Followed the road to the Souiac for 6 miles when we struck the river a little above the upper settlement. We followed it down for a mile and a half then crossed it and turned S. for 3 miles, at the end of a mile and a half from where we lay we passed another brook the course N. This and the other two brooks, which we passed last night, are as we were informed, branches of the Souiac, these brooks are not at present, either of them sufficiently large for mills, but we observed, they had been very high this spring. The Souiac had the same appearance where we first struck it, not holding 1/10th of the water which runs there early in the spring: from this I conclude there is a large tract of flat barrens near, of which I saw considerable quantities to the westward of the path from the middle river of Pictou to Souiac where I viewed the country from the tops of tall trees. The land along the road is chiefly soft wood till within 2 miles of the Souiac where it is chiefly pretty good hardwood. Great part of the softwood is spruce. In many places there is good building timber. In many others where the soil is a little worse, only small poles.

Soon after passing the Souiac we came upon Plaister of Paris ground which is everywhere full of holes, and deep round valleys, occasioned by the dissolving of the plaister below, leaving this we came upon very good hardwood hill, where there are large ledges of soft light blue slate. Upon these hill, there are more trees broken by the winds than in any place we have seen since we left Preston. All the hardwood we have passed between Pictou and this place, produced last year abundance of beech nuts although they failed everywhere else where we have been.

11th Proceeded S. for a mile and a half on hardwood land, then descended a large hill into a piece of swampy ground where there were a few holes like those made by Plaister of Paris and a spring about 20 feet long and 10 broad which had several plain well-trodden foot paths leading to it, made by the bears and which we perceived they had used many years, by the growing of the trees which they have bitten or scratched. The water has a blueish milky color, but when taken up in a cup, appears perfectly clear. It has no appearance of iron, but tasted somewhat like the water with which a gun is washed, or like bilge water, but without any taste of salt.

After walking about 10 rods westward in a bear path, we steered S. as exactly as possible for about a quarter of a mile when we struck a brook running S.W. which we passed and blazed a number of trees on the other side of it. We marked on N. and another S.E.

The brook here has no banks, we followed it for ½ a mile, it is a rapid torrent, and very soon has high banks, as the brook falls very fast. Where we left, its course is nearly W. and it has as we judged banks 150 feet high. We are informed by Mr. Henry that this branch of the Musquodoboit comes within a rod of the Souiac a mile or two above this spot. This brook joins the main branch of the Musquodoboit just above the Plaister of Paris rocks. We left the brook and proceeded S. about 3 miles when we struck the main branch about [??] of a mile above the great falls. The land very much broken partly hemlock and partly spruce thickets. The last mile rocky mountainous barrens. We followed the river down to Mr. Henry's about a mile and a half below the falls. From above a mile from where we struck the river, it falls very fast: the greatest fall in equal to about 15 feet perpendicular, and as we judged falls at an angle of about 45 degrees, the banks being in that place near 150 high, rocky and very steep. About half a mile still lower, we came to Plaister of Paris for a short distance, and then the interval begins. The banks were barren for some breadth, 'till we came to the Plaister. Mr. Henry informed us that there are very great quantities of iron ore in the hill which here lies on the W. side of the river. We observed iron ore in the loose stones of quartz which lay on the top of the ground.

<u>12th</u> Employed in providing for the woods.

<u>13th</u> Mr. Carter, being unwell we did not go till late in the day, when we steered S. from Col. Archibald's interval on burnt for a mile and a half. We then struck a small lake about a quarter of a mile long which has a brook running N. from the east end of it. We then discovered a perennial plant, which may possibly deserve to be ranked with hemp and flax if no material impediment should be found to dressing it. We stripped the bark from some of the last summers' stems, which stood erect, for a specimen, it appeared to be as fine and as strong as flax. That which had fallen down had lost all its strength. As it was not yet in flower I could not determine its genus, but think it to be a species of Indian hemp on silk grass (Arclepias). It grows on large branches from a perennial root, the stalks are about 3 feet high and a quarter of an inch diameter, much of it being without branches, but some stalks have two or four at top, it grows in a brook which runs in a bed of rocks resembling the brook which comes into Bedford Basin at the new bridge (Sackville) feet) except that it does not run rapidly. There is no earth within reach of its roots, except a little mud brought by the stream. It grows together with the black berried elder (?sumbucus) and scarlet winter berry (prines). The tops of the roots are at present about one inch under water; the brook being now about a middling height. I have seen many places on the edges of lakes, swamps and brooks, which appear suitable for this plant.

<u>14th</u> Proceeded S. 8 miles. The land ¾ burnt barrens, almost impassable in some places as the old growth of woods has fallen to the ground, no soil but a rock covered a few inches with turf. For the first 3 miles the rock is slate, afterwards the common mountain stone, the remaining [??] mostly

hardwood lying insulated unconnected pieces of from 20 to 150 acres usually rising a few feet above the level of the barrens, the soil rather poorer than is usual for hardwood. No remarkable hills or valleys as either of the barrens or hardwood land. At night we struck a brook the size of Tremain's (feet) about a mile below a lake which is 2 miles long and whose head is half a mile W. of our course. We frequently had prospects for 4 or 5 miles on different point, the land appeared to be much the same as that we were upon, and which consisted of small islands of hardwood in a burnt barren. We saw some salmon and abundance of Gaspereaus in this brook.

15th We followed the brook for about 3 miles the coast a little N. of S. when we found a tall spruce from which I could see a considerable distance.

To the S. lies a hill about 5 miles off which on that point is burnt naked, but has hardwood extending eastward 2 miles. To the E. at the distance of 5 miles there is hardwood for the breadth of a mile and a half. I could see S.E. for about 6 miles all barrens. W. 10 S. no hill to intercept my view and as far as I could see the land had the appearance of barrens, no hardwood of any value near us. From this spruce tree, we went W. 10 N. for a mile, and struck the brook again, we followed the same course for ½ a mile when it turned S.W. we then left it and proceeded W. for a mile and struck another brook about the size of Tremain's (feet) the course of it S. where we encamped. Here it has 40 or 50 acres of poor low interval on it, which produced a considerable quantity of blue joint grass. As we saw gaspereaus here, there must be something of a lake above. I should think that the sources of this brook and other branch likewise are within 2 or 3 miles of the Musquedoboit River, if I may judge from the shape of the land and the course of the small rivulets we which we passed. At 2 or 3 miles from Col. Archibald's we, passed a barren plain, which we could see extended several miles to the eastward and westward. It appears to be higher than the greater part of the land near it, and is in many places only covered with moss, without woods being very wet and springy. We had crossed the same plain the 12th of May at the distance of 3 or 4 miles from Geddess Mill. The brook we here encamped upon appears to join the other branch about one mile to the southward of this place.

16th Lay all day on account of rain.

17th Proceeded W. 4 miles the land began to be more hilly and the rocks larger, as we had no hopes of finding any valuable trace of land, after what we had seen. Mr. Carty being well acquainted with the land on the sea coast we resolved to make the best of our way to Musquedoboit. We steered different courses, to avoid the burnt land as much as possible till we struck a large lake and some rivulets, at the head of little river about 5 or 6 miles above where it empties into Musquedoboit having comes as we judged about 5 miles on a N.W. course, after we left going W. the lake and brooks we did not much notice supposing that they will be better described by Col. Archibald. The land is chiefly rocky barrens till after we passed the above mentioned lake, it then changes to fine sand with very little stone which continues to the Musquedoboit, the tops of some of the hills appear as barren as the rocky barrens, but the greater part is covered with a thick growth of hemlock, spruce, fir, poplar, and pine of a small size but tall. This kind of land when cleared is very light and mellow, and produces 2 or 3 very good crops, but soon becomes exhausted unless manured. The soil is composed of the same kind of sand with a mixture of loam for 10 or 12 miles down (as far as I have been there) on this side of the Musquodoboit but it is in the other parts generally richer than the spot which I now immediately describe. The soil varies much in color, being in the best places where the timber is hardwood of a dark color, especially where there is limestone, but on the poorest soft wood hills it is almost white, I have no doubt this soil is suitable for hemp. From all that we could learn from numbers of people who had traversed this part of the country, as well as from what we saw, I think there is reason to conclude that there is no considerable trace of land fit for cultivation anywhere near our route from Musquodoboit to St. Mary's till we were within 8 miles of the latter. From the place where we struck the river to the entrance of the other branch (a distance of about 14 miles upon a straight course) there is everywhere a hardwood hill on the western side of the river which appears of a better quality at the Fork than it is where we first struck the river, it probably continues till near the mouth. I was informed by a hunter that after going six miles up the brook which empties into Liscomb Harbour, he came into very good hardwood land in which he went up 3 miles farther and could not then see any softwood near. From the information we received from several different persons who had traversed the woods as well as from what we saw, I think there is reason to conclude that the whole of the land between the fork of St. Mary's, Milford Haven and the head of Antigonish is good and fit for cultivation and a very great part suitable for hemp. The land on Blanchard's road, which we followed to Pictou was for 6 or 8 miles limestone land, tolerably fertile, but very rocky, but as the road is generally on a high ridge, I think the land must have been better and more free from stone, at some distance from it on each side.

Before I conclude I must observe that we always received the most friendly treatment from every person we met with in our journey.

(Signed) Titus Smith

Halifax,
June 19th, 1801,
To His Excellency Sir John Wentworth Bart.

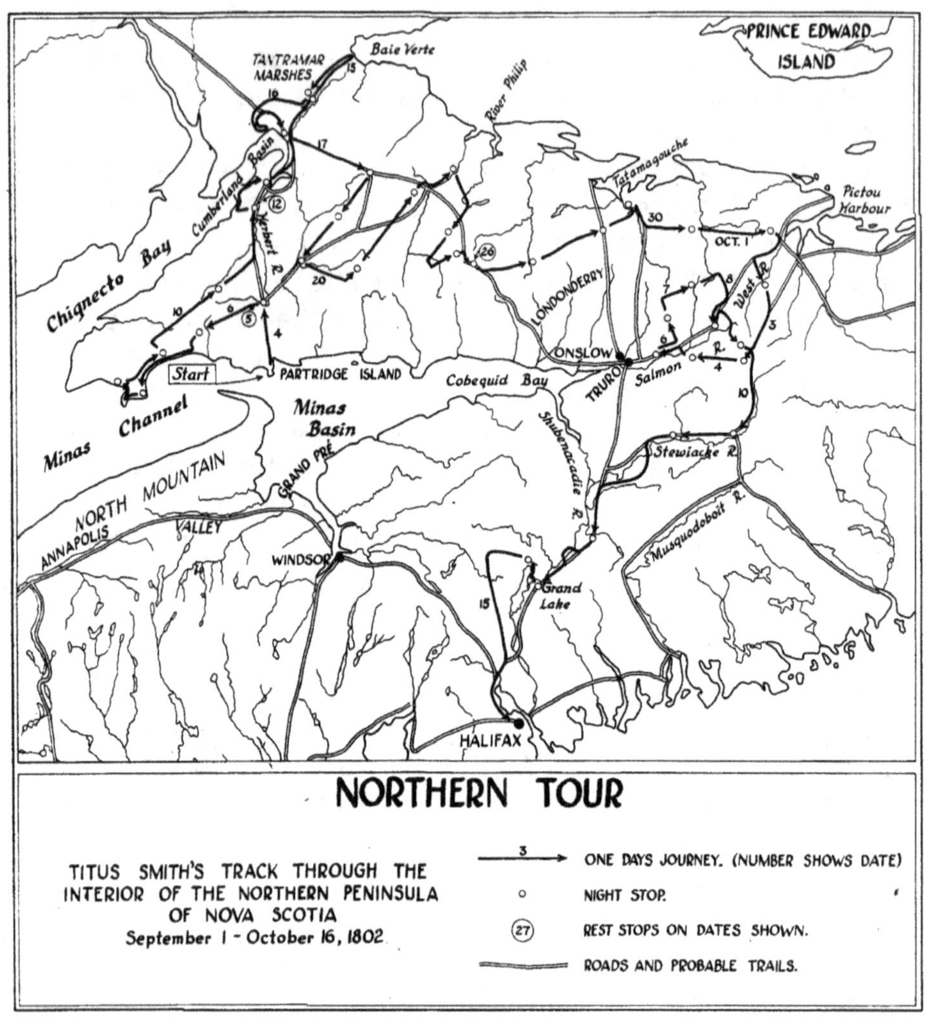

43 days
416 miles

THE NORTHERN TOUR

September 1st., 1802

<u>2 and 3</u>   Set out from Halifax and proceeded to Windsor. Detained for want of a passage.

<u>4th</u>   Proceeded to Mr. Lewis's, who lives 9 or 10 miles from Partridge Island, on the Cumberland road.

The land along this road is chiefly spruce and poor, the hardwood hills have a mixture of spruce, there is but very little stone in this land, near the shore I observed some slate. The Partridge Island river which lies by the side of the road is not above 8 miles long from the lake, on its head there is a portage of about 30 rods to a lake which empties into the principal stream of the river Hebert, there is a considerable fall in each of the streams before they reach the tide.

<u>5th</u>   Stayed at Mr. Lewis's.

<u>6th</u>   Left Mr. Lewis's and travelled N. for 10 miles. Land about half covered with beech, which has a mixture of spruce, the other half spruce from 6 to 16 inches diameter, with some mixture of hardwood. No swamps. Scarcely any stones. Soil is a reddish brown loam mixed with gravel-- generally dry--The greatest proportion of gravel in the spruce land. The stones are pebbles of a chocolate brown part of which are freestone, and part Argillaceous. Hills very high with frequent steep sided valleys, from 100 to 200 feet deep. At the end of five miles passed a brook size of Freshwater, course N. had before passed several rivulets, running the same way. At the end of 8, 9, and 10 miles passed 3 streams size of Freshwater, course S--at the end of one mile from Mr. Lewis's observed the N.E. end of Chepody mountain to bear W. 20 N. The land for 10 miles distance of

courses between N. and N. 30 E. appears to be a mixture of hardwood and large spruce. A valley at the distance of 7 miles appears to extend a long way S. W. and N. W. the hill beyond it is almost of an uniform height without swells.

7th   Proceeded a S. W. course for 2 miles then S. for 1½ miles, and struck the Bay about halfway from Partridge Island to Cape Dore. Proceeded to Cape Dore.

There is a great proportion of poor land just upon the coast than what there is farther back.

The land is very high in general along the shore with frequent deep steep sided valleys running back for a mile or more, which must prove a great impediment to making a road near the shore. The bank is generally rock, often 200 feet high, and so steep that it is impassable. The rock in some places is slate, which has in general a serpentine grain, in others the common mountain stone, and in others a mixed granite stone.

These rocks appear to be slowly decaying, they lie in Laminae, which are inclined at all angles from nearly horizontal to nearly perpendicular.

8th   Detained part of the day by the tide, went round the Cape and thence to Mr. Nolton's at Advocate Harbour, who as I had been informed was well acquainted with the woods near here--learned from him that the land is good from Cape Dore to Cape Chignecto for about 4 miles northward: farther north it is barren. The shore of Cumberland Bay is also barren for a considerable distance about apple river. There is only one place between Advocate Harbour and Cape Chignecto where the bank can be ascended, on account of the steepness of the rock, which is often 100 yards high, but a very small proportion of the land in the Parsbro district has been cleared as yet, it produces very good wheat which has never suffered much by any kind of blast or rust. There is a very great quantity of good spruce timber in this district which has a straighter grain than the spruce in some other parts of the province, it is easily split in fencing rails, shingles, clapboards, etc. Cape Dore has a rough rock bank often nearly perpendicular which I am told has been found by measuring with a line to be 30 yards high. It is rough gritty stone with veins of quartz and red or sky blue hornstone.   Copper is to be found both in the veins of quartz and in the solid rock, generally in small pieces of not more than the weight of a drachma: larger pieces are found among the loose stones at low water mark: the largest which I saw weighed 1 ½ pounds. It is to be found in the cliff very near the top, as well as at the bottom. Every piece of copper of any considerable size has the same irregular figure the metal will take when thrown in a state of fusion upon the ground. I think that this rock has been formerly melted at some remote period by a volcanic fire as the copper which is confined in solid rock, could not have formed as native copper is most frequently by water which has copper vitriol dissolved in it, meeting with iron ore. The rock is very frequently full of globose cavities from 1/8 to 1/2 inch diameter made as I think by air-bubbles at the time the rock was in a fluid state. In most of the rocks these cavities are filled up with pebbles of quartz, or kind of stone which is known to be often of a late growth and to fill up small crevices in rocks of other kinds of stone, as I have in the course of my tour, since leaving Cape Dore found reason to think that there is coal almost everywhere in the North Eastern part of the province, which very often accompanied by a pyrite composed of sulphur and iron (a mineral which often takes fire spontaneously, when laid in heaps exposed to the air and as I have seen at Tatmagouche an ore which gives fine copper at the first melting, mixed with small veins of coal. I think it not very extravagant to suppose that a large body of these two inflammable substances (coal and sulphur ore) taking fire may have melted a body of rock which contained veins of copper ore, and have produced the present appearances at Cape Dore) I could not find the least speck of copper ore, in any stone at Cape Dore, unless specks of green rust from decayed copper should be so called. If there is any large quantity of copper here, I think it most probably that it is under the water. There is at Advocate Harbour a quarry of Red Freestone, but it is too soft for building, the soil about it is red sand and is fertile.

9th   Returned as far as Mr. Fraser's, who lives about 12 miles N. W. from Partridge Island, left the shore there and followed a path for 3 miles towards Apple River course generally N. W.

10th   Followed the path 2 miles farther then turned N. of 5 E. for 12 miles. Land (for 2 miles from Mr. Frazer's) high hills covered with a mixture of spruce and hardwood, and pretty good; next 5 miles nearly level: one third part a barren sandy soil, covered with small black spruce: remaining two thirds large spruce mixed with hardwood: soil dry and gravelly inferior to that of the hills near the shore. Spars larger than they are near the shore, being often 18 inches diameter. Remaining 8 miles, barren, level, land, soil gravel or sand, with a few small stones, covered in some places with small black spruce, in others with a mixture of white birch and spruce. At the end of 8 miles (from Mr. Fraser's) passed a brook size of Tremain's (   ) course N. in the bottom of this brook a quarry of hard and red freestone.

11th   Continued N. 75 E. for 7 miles, and struck the road 5 miles above the head of the tide on the river Hebert. Land, poor, of the same kind as last described, except that the last 1½ miles are hilly and that the land falls considerably-- followed the road for 9½ miles down the river, to Mr. Shipley's. The upland always poor, chiefly sand, next to the river; the best pieces are moist, with a mixture of clay covered with a growth of white birch, poplar, ashe, and white maple. As the land contains no stone to impede cultivation, much of it may be cultivated as the marshes will support cattle enough to manure considerable tracts of upland. Passed small rivulets almost every ½ mile till I struck the road course S. Half a mile above the tide, a brook size of Tremain's (   ) from the west falls into the River Hebert, and just below the head of the tide, a stream called Mulbrook, about the size of Sackville river (   ) from the W. falls into it, this last stream has some hardwood hills upon it.

<u>12</u>th   Stayed at Mr. Shipley's.

<u>13</u>th   Left Mr. Shipley's and went 3 or 4 miles N. W. to the coal mine at the Joggins, on the bank of Cumberland Bay. The bank here, for a number of miles, is a rock of freestone, of various kinds, much of which is suitable for grindstones, of which a great number are made here. The grindstone rock varies in hardness, color, and fineness of grain, it is usually grey, light blue, or reddish brown, it lies in layers about 8 feet thick and is naturally split into Laminae from one foot to 3 inches in thickness. Between the layers are layers of a very fine grained stone, which has more clay in its composition, and appears to contain sulphur as it decays fast in the air, and is, when decayed, considerably impregnated with copperas and allum, in places where it is sheltered from rain. Coal is to be seen for 3 or 4 miles along the bank in small veins often not more than 1 or 2 inches thick. There are 3 or 4 large veins the best of which may be about 4 feet thick; they are visible for 200 or 300 yards in length from low water mark to the top of the bank; they run in a straight line, the same course as the strata stone which they lie between, and which at the place where the large veins are rise at an angle somewhat less than 45 degrees from the plane of the horizon, they are nearly opposite Cape Maringuin, the coal also dips into the bank running under ground, at nearly the same angle with which it rises in the bank. This coal has too much sulphur ore mixed with it in general, for the use of smiths, although it burns very well: it is thought by some people, that by working deeper, the coal would be free from sulphur, but it will not be easy to work these veins to any great depth, on account of the smallness

of the veins, and the direction they run in. Came at night to Barrons field.

14th   Crossed the river and proceeded as far as Mr. Trenham's, on the road to Bay Verte.

15th   Went to Bay Verte, returned as far as Mr. Hewson's at Joli Coeur.

16th   Proceeded to Mr. Botsford's at Westcock, after conferring with him returned as far as Mr. J. Chipman's at Fort Lawrence. There is no very high land between Cumberland Bay and Bay Verte, the soil is everywhere sandy with a sufficient mixture of loam to make a very muddy road. The Portage Lake on the head of the Missiquash is about 3 miles from the marsh at Bay Verte and 3½ miles from the landing place. Small rivulets which fall into this lake and others which fall into Bay Verte may be found within a mile of each other. I should think that the water from the Portage Lake might be carried to Bay Verte by a ditch in no place more than 12 feet deep. It is not less than 5 miles from that part of the Portage Lake which is nearest to Bay Verte to the head of the tide in the Missiquash: most of this distance is dead water, in a swamp, there being but little fall. I saw no rocks going to the Bay Verte, but only a few loose stones of freestone, but think it probably there may be quarries of freestone, at some depth not much beneath the level of low water, as it is seen to be in the bed of the river at Barrons field. I am informed that a stream of the Tignish (which empties into Bay Verte, about 3 miles S. E. of the place where the road strikes it) comes very near the La Plance River (which runs through the Amherst marshe and lies 2 or 3 miles S. E. of the Missiquash) but that the tide waters do not come so near each other as in the passage by the Missiquash.

The La Plance is but a small brook of fresh water. Old Lao river, which runs through the great marsh of Tantramar is a larger river than Missiquash and heads in lakes and morasses, near the head of the marsh. The tide would reach 8 or 10 miles up this river. The land is low between the head of this river and Bay Verte. I am informed that the Bay Verte is shoal with a muddy bottom and that vessels cannot come nearer than 9 miles to the landing place, that there is a channel of deep water but so narrow and crooked that it cannot be followed. The depth of water here, I suppose, may be learned from Des Barres charts. I learn from Mr. Botsford that the highest customary spring tides are, at Cape Chignecto, 115 feet; at Cape Enrage, 50 feet; at the head of Cumberland Bay 55 feet; at Bay Verte from 8 to 10 feet. A strong S. W. will sometimes make the spring tides at Cumberland 5 or 6 feet higher than usual. The usual tides at Cape Chignecto are 36 feet, at Cape Enrage 40 feet, at Cumberland 45 feet, and at Bay Verte 6 feet. The tides at Bay Verte are about 3 hours earlier than at Cumberland, they are much more irregular, and the time of high water is supposed to depend upon the wind and the current of the St. Lawrence. The time of high water at Cumberland, they are much more irregular, and the time of high water at Cumberland is about 3 hours, 20 minutes later than at Halifax. Mr. Botsford supposes the half tide at Cumberland to be nearly upon a level with that of Bay Verte: he thinks the consequence of opening a communication between them would be to lower the tides and lessen the current in the Bay of Fundy, as he conceives the usual height of the tides to be owing to the force of a current caused by the length of the Bay, and the narrowing of its bank towards the head notwithstanding the length of time that this part of the province has been settled, I think it contains but a small part of the inhabitants which it is capable of supporting. A great proportion of the marsh is still undrained, and does not produce anything near what it would it if were in good order, as the owners possess such tracts that they have not been able to pay a proper attention to them. The upland about here possesses the great advantage of being free from stones: some parts of it have a very barren sandy soil--some tracts are chiefly loam and very good but the quarter part is a mixture of sand and loam, though not sufficiently fertile in its present condition to produce large crops is capable of making good land by being manured, and a large quantity of upland may certainly be manured from the large produce of such a large quantity of fertile marsh, which never needs any recruit. The inhabitants in general appear to be sensible that their lands, may be greatly improved, but as they have been able to support themselves well from the lands, in their present condition, the great difficulty of procuring labourers has prevented them from making any very rapid improvements. They expect that the peace will furnish them with more hands. They are now raising a subscription for the purpose of making a direct road from Fort Lawrence to Fort Cumberland, as the present road is very circuitous: to effect this they intend to make a new Abatdeau about 2 miles below where the present road crosses the Missiquash, which besides materially shortening the road will save the expense of supporting a dyke, on each side of the river for 2 miles.

17th   Left Mr. Chapman's and proceeded 15 miles along the Cobequid road to Colburn's at a brook of the Macau; not larger than the Freshwater river (   ) 7 miles back from Coburns, had crossed the Napan, which is a considerable stream and has some interval upon it. The land frequently changes its quality along this road; the soil is generally sand, mixed more or less with loam. Half this land is very poor, covered with spruce of a small size, some part of the remainder (in small tracts) very good, covered with an old growth, containing a considerable quantity of hard maple: the residue moist land, covered with white beech, fir, poplar, and white maple, in many places a mixture of ashe, much of this is pretty good for grass. I am informed that the land from the Bay Verte to Ramsheg is generally better near the coast, than it is at some distance back. There being a considerable tract of heavy timbered land near the coast a road which is projected from the head of Amherst marsh to strike the coast within a few paces of the mouth of the River

Philip will, as it is said, pass through considerable tracts of good land, in which there is a large quantity of wild meadow. There is, notwithstanding, a large tract of very barren land near the source of the Napan. Through all this sandy country there are frequent quarries of freestone, varying in fineness and hardness. It appears to be the common soil cemented together, where that is gravelly, as is sometimes the case. Pebbles of the same kind are found in the stone, it is generally a light blue or gray color, sometimes reddish, and in some places of a dark brick color, this last is very hard and fine grained and the soil near it usually has a considerable mixture of clay.

18th   Left the road at Macan brook and proceeded S. 55 W. for 7 miles. Land for the first 3½ miles a spruce thicket, with some mixture of white birch and poplar. Last 3½ miles, a burnt barren, generally covered (before the fire) with spruce, in some places with yellow and mountain pine, the burnt lane extends as far as 3 miles southward of my course, N. I could not see it above one mile as the land rises that way.

19th   Continued S. 55 W. for 8 miles and struck the east brook of Macan, about ½ mile from where it falls into that river which is at the bridge, when the Partridge Island road crossed that stream 9 miles from Lewis's, and 13 from where the Napan falls into the Macan. The brook which crosses the road at Colbourne empties into the river 5 miles below this place. The east brook which empties in here reaches to within 3 miles S. E. of my course, most of the way: land this day all bad till within 1½ miles of the road, when it grows hilly and is covered with large trees, spruce, hemlock, pine, and some hardwood, with swamps which are worth draining. Soil still chiefly sand mixed with loam in the best places. This morning observed hills, at the distance of 8 miles, south and southwest: land apparently covered with small spruce till near the hills. Stone still freestone of various kinds.

There is limestone at the junction of the Napan and Macan and Plaister at Amherst point.

20th   Left the road and travelled S. 35 E. for 7 miles. The first mile along the river, which I then left of the land hand turned N. 55 E. for 3 miles. Land for the first 3 miles covered chiefly with spruce with a small mixture of hardwood, and a few large pines: next two miles, a mixture of hemlock, spruce, and hardwood, last 5 miles, almost all hardwood, on high hills, soil gravelly, but in general of good strength everywhere stone: some pieces so stony as to be incapable of being ploughed--stones composed of pebbles of various kinds cemented together. At the end of 2½ miles passed a brook size of Freshwater (   ) which empties into Macan near the road. At the end of 5½ miles, passed another same size, course N. at the end of the 8 and 8½ two more, same size, course W. There are near these brooks some groves composed almost entirely of hard maple where the Macan people make considerable quantities of sugar. They inform me that a ridge of hardwood runs from here to port [?] Oceonomie.

21st   Continued N. 55 E. for 12 miles. Land for 3 miles nearly all hardwood, next mile spruce, then for 6 miles alternately hardwood and mixed land. One third of this 6 miles very good the remainder of an inferior quality. Soil somewhat stone, everywhere gravelly with a mixture of loam generally dry. Last two miles land which has formerly been burnt, covered in some places with spruce, in others with a mixture of white birch, poplar and spruce. Soil a mixture of sand and clay, poor but neither so stony nor so gravelly as the hardwood land. About 1/8 of this land is moist and swampy and much better than dry land. There are some quarries of freestone in this land. At the end of 1½ miles, 2 miles, and 5 miles, passed brooks size of Freshwater (   ) course N. W. The land falls that way for the first 9 miles with rivulets running N. W. every [? ¾] of a mile in deep steep sided valleys. For the last 3 miles the land falls to the southeast.

22nd Continued N. 55 E. for 2 miles and struck the road 2½ miles N. W. of the River Philip followed the road to the river and went 4 miles down the river to the salt spring. Land covered with spruce and white birch, soil, sand, and gravel mixed often with clay, hills not high. The intervals on the River Philip is good, and produced large crops. The principal salt spring rises upon the land side of the interval at the distance of a quarter of a mile from the river: it is now weaker than usual owing to the late heavy rains, but it tastes salter then sea water. I am told that 3 gallons of this water have yielded above a quart of salt. From the taste of the water I should think it to contain an unusual proportion of bittern salt. There are several springs near each other which together with fresh water from a pond of near an acre, which is salter in dry weather than the sea. Samphire and other sea plants grow about the pond, the water from it forms a marsh yields about 15 tons of salt hay, chiefly flat grass. Other salt springs rise in different places in the interval within 50 rods of this. A stream which turns a mill here (and which rises in plaister ground within a mile of the salt spring) is a little salt, it is about 2 miles from here to where the tide backs the freshwater, a rapid current all the way. The upland by the side of which this spring rises is low and very barren. I am informed that there is no good land between here and Ramsheg upon a direct course, that a hardwood ridge runs back a few miles from the sea between the River Philip and Pugwash and that there is a considerable body of hardwood and heavy timbered land, along the shore between Pugwash and Ramsheg. About ½ mile below the salt spring of the River Philip, there is a vein of poor salty coal about 6 inches thick.

23rd Crossed the river and travelled S. E. for 5 miles, then S. 55 W. for 5 miles farther. Land for the first 4 miles on a little rising from the river, sandy soil generally very poor, covered with small spruce. Some pieces better with a mixture of hemlock, birch, fir, and white cedar, and a few good swamps, next 3 miles white birch and poplar, along a ridge which is not greatly elevated above the valleys. Last 3 miles, sandy barrens and swamps, covered with black spruce. At the end of 7 miles observed the land to be low and covered apparently with spruce for 6 or 8 miles or to the foot of the Cobequid mountain on a south and southeast course, one mile before I halted passed a brook larger than Tremain's (   ) W.

24th   Continued S. 55 W. for 5 miles, and struck a branch of the River Philip about half the size of Sackville River (   ) course N. W. crossed and went S. W. for one mile then S. for ½ mile then E. for 2 miles and struck the river again, crossed it and went E. 20 N. for 2 miles farther. The river lies just at the foot of the Cobequid mountains. The hill S. W. of the river is very high all hardwood. Somewhat stone. The hill sides very good, tops of the hills less fertile, soil gravel and a mixture of loam. Land till I struck the river, alternately spruce plains and hills covered with a mixture of hard and soft wood. Soil but ordinary, a few small tracts excepted. From the place where I first struck the river, it is about 1½ miles to where it united with the other branch. The hardwood hill on the western side of the River Philip reaches about a mile lower than where these two branches unite. At the place where I first passed the river there is a quarry of soft freestone, in which I saw some small veins of coal, and ½ mile before I repassed this river I saw in a small brook a quarry of freestone likewise containing coal. The veins are not more than ½ inch thick and have larger quantities of Sulphur ore adjoining them.

25th   Continued N. 70 E. for 2 miles and struck the road, followed it for 3 miles to Mr. Purdy's who lives 17 miles from Londonderry village and 9 from the River Philip at the foot of the mountain. A small brook of the River Philip crossed the road here, course west. From where I left the river to Mr.

Purdy's the land is covered with a mixture of hard and soft wood--soil generally but ordinary. Stones mostly of the freestone kind. The valley which runs from here to Ramsheg is generally covered with spruce, much of it very poor, but there is some moist places, which are good, and some valuable wild meadows. The interval on the Ramsheg river is, as I am informed, very good and equal to that of the River Philip.

I have followed the road for 5 miles S. E. and observed that this mountain is almost entirely hardwood, which continues as I am informed nearly to Londonderry and Oceonomie; it is a body of hills intersected by deep valleys running in various directions, each of them containing a small brook. The waters of the River Philip come chiefly from these hills. The soil is commonly gravelly with a mixture of loam, it is stony though not more than a fourth part of it has so much stone as materially to impede cultivation, this land is chiefly pretty dry. There are some pieces of very good land here, but the greater part of the mountain is but of a middling quality.

The growth of timber is short partly owing to the elevated situation: it is everywhere choaked up with a thick underwood. Grain and potatoes grow very well upon these hills.

These hills are probably solid rock, covered for a considerable depth with earth as the naked rock often appears on the tops of the highest hills and in brooks. The rock is part coarse millstone granite, the sparry part of which is red, part of black and white hard rock chiefly composed of Silecious spar. It will be difficult to make roads here on account of the frequency and steepness of the valleys, some of which are equal to 100 yards perpendicular descent. The highest land here is the Sugar loaf hill about 1½ miles N. W. from Mr. Purdy's, it is used for a sea mark in coming over from Prince Edward Island. These hills appear the higher from the lowness of the country towards Cumberland and the Gulph of St. Lawrence. I should not think the highest hill to be 1000 feet above the sea level. From a hill 2 miles S. E. of Mr. Purdy's near the road, the N. E. end of the Chepody mountain bears N. 50 W. and Tatmagouche Bay N. 75 E.

26th   Remained at Mr. Purdy's.

27th   Followed the road 1½ miles S. E. to the top of the hill, then left it and went N. 85 E. for 6 miles, then E. for 2 miles, land of the same quality as has already been described for the mountain. At the end of 2 and 5 miles passed 2 brooks size of Freshwater (   ) besides several smaller, course of all N. At the end of the 6 miles observed Cape Tormentine to bear N. 75 E. The Cape on the W. side of Tatmagouche Bay bears N. 70 E., could not see Prince Edward Island; the valley which bounds the mountain lies from ½ mile to 2 miles north of my course.

28th Continued E. for 10 miles, first 4 miles on the mountain, remainder of the plain. 2 miles before I halted, observed the mountain to lie one mile S. of my course. Land on the mountain the same as before except that it is more stony and that the valleys are deeper, owing to my travelling just on the brow. The summit of the highest hills on the brow of the mountain, where they are much exposed to the wind are covered with a growth of scrubbed ash, hard maple, and hornbeam, with an underwood of Choackcherry and wild currants; land on the plain generally poor, covered with hemlock and spruce, mixed in some places with hardwood, some good ashe swamps. No hills more than 10 feet above the valleys--first two miles very stony and gravelly--last 4 miles less stony, soil sand--some quarries of freestone are to be seen in the brooks; at the end of two miles passed a brook size of Tremain's (   ). At the end of 5 and 8 miles passed two others size of Freshwater (   ) besides many smaller streams, course of all N. At the end of 3 miles observed Cape Tormentine to bear N. 2 W. The Cape west side of Tatmagouche N. 65 E.

<u>29th</u>   Continued E. for 6 miles, and struck the road at the place where a small [?] called Miracle brook empties into the [? East] river of Tatmagouche 3½ miles above its junction with the other river. Three miles back had passed this river, they are each about the size of Sackville River (   ). At the end of 3 miles observed the mountain to be [? 3] miles S. of my course, my course always on the plain, land poorer than where I travelled yesterday, swamps, black spruce. The upland has on it a great quantity of pine, much of which is good for boards, but very little of it is fit for most timber. There is a little interval on the rivers. Followed the road down for 1½ miles to Mr. A. Waughs, am informed that the land is all low between here and Pictou, generally poor and covered with spruce but mixed with many [? small] pieces of good land, that there is a piece of good land on the west side of Caribou Harbour, and a large tract which his very barren about half way from Caribou to the River St. John. I am told that small veins of coal accompanied with Sulphur ore, are to be seen in many places in the quarries of freestone, in the beds of the brooks here; when the waters are low. Mr. Waugh has seen loose pieces of coal 5 inches thick in the river below his house. At the mouth of Mirehole brook I had been informed a number of barrels of ore had been formerly taken out and that there was a large body of one there, I could not ascertain the truth of this, as to the quantity of ore as the water was so high, that I could not see the place from whence it was taken, and I saw no persons here who knew what quantity of ore is to be seen there at present, although they knew that a considerable quantity had been dug out of this place. The rock here is a coarse freestone stained with verdigris in some places; by breaking one of the stones in the bank I collected a little of the ore, which had about an equal quantity of coal sticking to it.

This ore is a very soft sand of black lead or dark steel color. It does not appear to contain Sulphur or [? arsenic]. Upon melting the ore with salt peter (a method which always wastes a part of the metal) 33 grains of the ore yielded 13 grains of fine copper. It would probably yield half its weight in copper if it were [? assayed] in a way that would save all the metal.   If a large quantity can be found it must prove a valuable ore, as it fusses easily and yields very fine malleable copper at the first melting which is not the case with most copper ores.

30th   Left Mr. Waugh's and followed the road for 4 miles, course a little W. of S., then left it and steered S. 60 E. for 5 miles, directly after leaving the road passed a brook size of Tremain's (   ) course N., which at this place receives a brook size of Freshwater from the west. At the end of one mile (from the road) passed the principal stream of the West River, which has here about 40 rods of interval. At the end of 2 miles and 4 miles from the road passed two brooks size of Freshwater besides a number of smaller trees, course of all northward. Land for 6 miles from Mr. Waugh's, low, covered generally with a mixture of hardwood and hemlock: soil, sand and loam. Last 3 miles, on the mountain almost all hardwood, very good. The trees are very tall, with abundance of large maple. The hills are not very steep nor very high, except the last where I halted. Banks of the brooks very steep generally equal to 25 or 30 feet perpendicular: soil, gravel and loam of reddish color. Land a little stony--stones mostly pebbles of a light chocolate color.

Oct. 1st   Continued S. 60 [?S] for 9 miles, then E. for 1½ miles to a house within 2 miles of the West River, and 3 miles above the tide. Land for the first 2 miles chiefly hardwood on the mountain, next 4 miles on the plain the hills being left on the right, hemlock land. Soil, sand and loam, half poor with a mixture of hardwood on the hills, which are not very high here, very good soil, loam, abundance of ash, hard maple and hornbeam-- last 2½ miles chiefly hardwood--Soil dry gravelly and stoney. Land very rough with small steep hills, the tops of which are covered with hemlock. At the end of 2 miles passed a brook size of Freshwater (   ) course [? east] several lesser brooks, same course. At the end of [? 3] miles a stream size of Tremain's (   ) course N. At the end of the 6 and 7 miles 2 brooks size of Freshwater (   ) course N. I am told by people acquainted with the woods that these brooks all belong to the River John and none of them to Caribou: for the last 2 miles the rivulets run S. The brooks this day have generally high steep banks.

2<u>nd</u>   Followed a path a S. E. course for 2 miles to the road: followed the road S. W. along the river for 2 miles farther to Mr. Connels. After having some bread made followed the road, which here leaves the river for 3 miles, then steered S. for 3 miles. Half a mile before I came to Mr. Connell's, passed a brook size of Freshwater (   ). 2 miles after leaving Mr. Connell's passed a stream containing nearly half the West River coming from the west. A brook size of Freshwater falls into it at the same place coming from the northwest. One mile after leaving the road passed the other branch of the West River at the Salt Works, the salt springs rise here by the side of the river, separated from it only by a bank of gravel and are not a foot above its present level. The spring which is worked and which is separated by a wall from the Freshwater, has yielded in a dry season as I am informed three packs of fine salt from a barrel of water-- Coal is found in small quantities along the river and most of the brooks which fall into it, as they frequently run upon a bed of freestone. The best coal has been found within a mile of the West River, on the west side of it just against the head of the tide. It appears for a considerable distance upon the top of the ground covered only with turf and is as I am informed free of Sulphur: The low land next the river is commonly sandy and covered with hemlock and spruce; the hills back of this land are hardwood with a soil of reddish brown loam mixed with gravel.

The stones near the river are chiefly grey free stones: there are some rocks in the banks composed of small pebbles cemented together by quartz or freestone. The last mile which I travelled this day, a good hardwood hill.

3rd Proceeded S. for 5 miles, and struck the foot path from the middle river to Souiac: followed its course as I judged south 50 west for 8 miles. Land for the first 9 miles hardwood of a poor quality: trees small and mossy, often mixed with fir and hemlock. Soil, a pale yellow, gravelly with a considerable quantity of small stones--hills not high, many flat moist places, and a number of small swamps which are good for grass. Last 4 miles more plain through it lies pretty high: half covered with a mixture of hardwood and large spruce: the other half wholly spruce, the greater part of which is of a size fit for timber. Soil moist and stiff, but poor, without cradle hills, less stony (some small spots excepted) than the hardwood which I passed in the morning. Stones millstone granite, slate, and the hard blue mountain stone--The brooks have not high banks, and the stones in the bottom of them, are covered with a black ivory crust. For the first 3 miles all the rivulets ran east: then in the 4th mile passed 2 or 3 running west. Half a mile after striking the footpath passed a brook the size of Freshwater ( ) and 4 miles farther another of the same size course of both S. E. -- at the end of 8 miles observed the land to be hardwood with some mixture of softwood for 3 miles S. E., observed a valley which lay ½ mile S. E. to run 4 or 5 miles N. E. and within a mile of my station to be joined by another long valley from the south. At the end of 12 miles observed the hills from the distance of 6 miles upon courses between S. E. and S. W. to be a mixture of hardwood and spruce, the valleys are therefore probably all spruce. Land highest towards the N. W. as it has been all along this path. Mountains from N. W.

to N. in view at a distance. High land S. W. supposed to be between the heads of Souiac and [? Muscuedoboit.]

4th   Left the footpath and steered N. 65 W. for 8 miles. Land very flat for the first 7 miles, hills seldom more than 20 feet above the valleys. Land one third covered with a growth of large spruce mixed with hardwood--[? 1/3] covered with spruce of a size fit for timber--[? 1/3] mossy swamps and barrens covered with small black spruce. Last mile passed over a considerable hill of good hardwood land, soil for the first 5 miles, pale gravelly, often still with a kind of slate clay--last 3 miles it changed to a reddish brown. At the end of one mile passed a brook size of Freshwater (   ) course S. W. ½ a mile farther another same size and course-- At the end of 7 miles a third, same size, course N--at end of 3 miles observed the land for 1 mile N. 30 E. to N. 40 W. at the end of 5 miles observed the land to be mostly spruce for 5 miles upon courses between N. 10 E. and N. W. and for one mile every other way. At the end of 7 miles land chiefly spruce for 3 miles S. and S. W. hardwood for 2 miles N. W. high mountains in view from N. 65 W. to N.

The rivulets for the first 4 miles run south, last four miles they run N. Some places this day are almost covered with stones but the land in general is not very stony--stones slate and blue mountain stone.

5th   Proceeded N. 15 W. for 3 miles, and struck the road 10 miles from Onslow and 19 from Mr. Connel's at Pictou. At the end of one mile passed Salmon River in a valley which I should judge to be 500 feet below the general level of the land, I was upon yesterday. Land for the first mile hardwood good soil but stony, next 2 miles half barren spruce swamps, half hills covered with a mixture of hemlock and hardwood, soil a red sandy loam--followed the road for 4½ miles towards Onslow to Mr. Christies, the road followes a ridge of hardwood and hemlock, the soil grows more sandy as it approaches the shore. Where I passed Salmon River there are some rocks of coarse hard freestone and others of a fine grained blue and chocolate colored stone which appears to decay fast, and from the reddish loam above mentioned, which is in some places of a brick red, lower down the river are some quarries of soft red sand stone of the same kind as that at St. Mary's Bay and Advocate Harbour.

6th   Left Mr. Christie's and returned 4½ miles back, to where I struck the road yesterday: from there proceeded North for 4 miles. Land all poor most of it very stony. Soil generally of a pale color, the land is about half covered with thickets of small spruce and fir and small swamps the remainder a mixture of large spruce hemlock and scrubbed hardwood: the hardwood mostly on the tops of the hills, which are not very high above the valleys although the land lies pretty high above the sea level; at the end of 3 miles observed that the land was mostly spruce on a easterly course for 5 miles--N. 60 W. hardwood mixed with spruce as far as I could distinguish the timber--N. 20 W. The mountain appears to be within 5 or 6 miles. N. W. a hardwood hill within 1½ miles. At the end of 2 miles passed Onslow River about the size of Tremain's brook (   ) stones, wholly the blue mountain stone.

7th   Continued N. for 3 miles, then turned E. and proceeded 5 miles. First 1½ rising a hill after which the land is almost all hardwood. Half a mile before I turned E. passed two brooks size of Freshwater (   ) course west, within 40 rods of each other. The hills within ½ mile of these brooks, on each side, are good land, the remainder is land of good strength, but more than half of it is so rocky that it will only answer for pasturage: many places are moist and good for grass. Timber mostly large yellow birch. Stones, millstone, granite, soil gravelly. One mile from where I turned E. passed a brook rather less than Freshwater (   ) course N. 2 miles farther another size of Tremains (   ) course S. At night struck a lake ¼ mile long, a small brook from it running N: At the place where I turned E. observed that one mile farther N. would reach the top of the mountain, it shows so many sudden swells that it is probably very rocky.

<u>8th</u>   Continued east for 4 miles then turned S. for 3 miles and struck the road [? 7] miles from Kingsleys, at Salmon River and 8 miles from McConnels--Proceeded to Salmon River. At the end of one and two miles passed 2 brooks size of Freshwater (   ) course N. half a mile before striking the road passed another, same size course east. Land all hardwood for the first 10 miles, much of it very good best on the two Tatamagouche brooks, none so stony but that it may be cultivated, last 4 miles a plain. Land half covered with spruce, the other half with a mixture of hardwood and softwood. Soil a reddish loam, rather poor in general. Half a mile before I struck the road the stones change from granite to a mixture of blue mountain stone slate, hard freestone and stones composed of small pebbles cemented together.

9th   Followed the road E. for 1½ miles then steered S. E. for 4 miles then S. for one mile then S. E. for 3 miles. At the end of 3 miles (from the road) passed a brook size of Freshwater (   ) course W. At the end of 4½ miles passed another size of Freshwater (   ) course N. of W. Land for the first 2½ miles (from the road) rough, hilly, and stony, a fourth part hardwood of an ordinary quality, the remainder thickets of small fir, spruce swamps and stony hills covered with hemlock and spruce--next 3 miles a barren mostly plain, much of which is swamp, covered with small black spruce-- last 2½ miles very high land, chief hardwood generally stony and of but an ordinary soil. One mile before I halted observed that the head of the book which I passed last was about one mile E. from me. Within ½ a mile of this is the head of a branch of the West River of Pictou which runs from there a north course, at the foot of a high hardwood hill which lies E. of it till it reaches a gap in the hill, bearing N. 30 E. at the distance of 3 or 4 miles from this gap the hardwood hill runs 7. The land between me and these hills is low and covered with spruce. Observed a hill covered with spruce at the distance of 2 miles S. W. A hardwood hill continues for several miles down the book I passed last, on the S. W. side. Soil till I padded the barren land, a reddish brown loam--last 2 miles, soil yellow, stones, slate and blue mountain stone.

10th   Proceeded S. for 3 miles and struck the path from the West River one mile E. of where I left it on the 4th October. First 1½ miles hardwood last 1½ miles almost all spruce swamps. Followed the path 10 miles to the N. branch of the Souiac, which is strikes about 21 miles from where the Cobequid road passed the Souiac. Followed the river down for 5 miles to Mr. R. Logan's--½ mile below here a brook size of Tremain's (   ) empties in on the N. side.

The S. branch joins the other 4 miles below Mr. Logan's (The dark color of the water in this branch shows it to come from spruce swamps) 5 miles below Mr. Logan's is a salt spring 9 miles below Mr. Logan's a brook size of Tremain's (   ) empties in on the N. side, and near the Cobequid road another, same size, on the north side also.

11th   Went 9 miles down the river went to see the salt springs, they rise in a large marsh, which lies ½ mile from the river on the N. side. The marsh may contain 100 acres and is covered with a mixture of blue joint and flat grass. (Flat grass usually grows on salt marshes when first dyked) it has also a blue clayed soil which would yield a great quantity, if it were thrown into dykes, as I found it strongly impregnated with alum, wherever the soil was heaped up by Musquashes. The flat grass tastes salt in all parts of the marsh. The principal salt spring is 40 or 50 rods from the upland, it is saltier than sea water, but could not be worked without considerable expense, as the back water from the river frequently flows the marsh. There is another large marsh within a mile of this which produces flat grass, and has in it springs which are a little salt. The land on the N.

side of the river, as far down as the salt spring is usually chiefly covered with soft wood, for 1 or 2 miles back from the river. Soil sand and clay--a hill lies north of this softwood land, which is covered with a mixture of hard and softwood. On the south side of the river the hardwood hill lies near the river down to the south branch below, this land is low and barren chiefly burnt over for several miles south from the river. There is plaister about 2 miles north from the salt spring, and limestone 4 miles lower down on the north side of the river. The interval on this river has a considerable mixture of sand in the soil and would probably answer well for hemp. Twenty bushels of wheat to the acre is acounted a very good crop, although it sometimes yields nearly thirty.

12<u>th</u>   Left the Souiac 8 miles above the road and went S. 20 West for 3 miles and then S. 70 W. till I struck St. Andrew's River (here about the size of Tremains brook (   ) 1½ miles above the road; followed it, course a little N. of W. to the road, followed the road 7 miles to Muir's at Gay's River. Land from the Souiac to within 1½ miles of St. Andrews, a poor burnt sandy plain originally covered with small spruce and pine timber; within 1½ miles of where I struck St. Andrew's there is a little plaister ground: from there to the brook the land is loamy, and something better than what I had passed before, though it is still burnt land; from where I struck St. Andrews, a hill covered with a mixture of hard and soft wood, on the southwest side of the brook reaches as far as I could see (about 4 miles to the S. E. I am told that this is a tolerable good piece of land for 5 miles breadth.

13<u>th</u>   Followed the road from Muir's to the Shubenacadie passed it and followed it up for 1½ miles, then repassed it, came to the road and followed it as far as Halls. The land near Shubenacadie is usually covered with a mixture of hardwood and soft, the soil is sand and loam, it is easily cultivated, but in most place needs manure. The interval is more suitable for grass than for arable land, it is very often flowed, owing to the tides which rise several feet for many miles above where the salt water reaches; and if the river is high at the spring tide, it always flows the interval on the west side of the Shubenacadie, near where I passed it, the land is a spruce plain and poor at the distance of a mile from the river and I am told that this kid of land reaches for several miles westward. I have been considerably delayed this day by being obliged twice to make rafts to pass the river. I am told that a bridge is to be erected, where I last passed the river. Is inhabited on both sides, and is not fordable.

14th   Followed the road which leads from Halls to the river for a mile to the bridge, passed the river and followed it for 2 or 3 miles to the Grand Lake, followed the lake for 4 miles to its N. end, course a little E. of N. Land always low, soil sand or clay in some places stony: timber usually hemlock, with a mixture of pine and spruce, below the lake there is a considerable tract which appears to have been once a lake, now sandy islands, parted by alder swamps, which have frequently creeks running through them. Near this place are a few of the tallest pines I have seen in this province. Within 2 miles of the N. end of the Grand lake, there is plaister on the east side which continues for a mile north. From where the Plaister begins to the north end of the lake, there is a little moist land generally, next lake bearing considerable ash and elm which is good grass land. The stream which falls into the N. end of the lake is about the size of Freshwater (   ) and may have 30 or 40 acres of low interval upon it, the water in this brook is very dark. The rapid parts of the Shubenacadie where I have been generally a low bank and river is shoal for the whole breadth, in such places I should think it best in clearing a passage for boats to make it next to the shore and to clear a path along the bank as it is of great service to have a man on shore with a rope in taking a heavy loaded boat against the current.

15th   Left the lake and proceeded N. W. for 8 miles, and struck the 9 mile river road 4½ miles beyond Currie's farm and 11½ miles beyond Beaver bank, followed the road to Currie's farm--Within a mile of the lake passed a little loamy hemlock land, which has some plaister pits in it: from thence to the road all spruce land, commonly very rocky, none of it fit for cultivation. At the end of 3 miles from the last passed a brook of the size of Tremain's (   ) course east. One mile beyond Currie's farm, another same size, course N. W.

16th   Returned home.

GENERAL OBSERVATIONS on the NORTHERN TOUR

In my tour through the Northeastern part of the province, I have observed that there is a ridge of high land which runs from Cape Chignecto to Pictou. The soil varies in different parts of this mountain, but it is almost everywhere worth cultivating. In the Parsborough district, there is a considerable mixture of spruce with the hardwood. The land is very free from stone, and generally dry. Wheat has succeeded well upon this land, and I have no doubt but it would procure good hemp, when in good pith as the soil is naturally mellow and loose, except close to the shore, where there is clay in some places. From the head of the Macan to Pictou, the mountain is generally covered with hardwood: the soil is commonly gravelly and always (more or less) stony. Those places which are most stony are moist, and most suitable for grass, but the greater part of this land is dry and has not so much stone in it as to be any considerable impediment to cultivation: Some parts of this land would answer well for hemp, but the greatest part is a soil which would not easily be made sufficiently mellow for that plant. From the mountain to Cumberland and the Gulf of St. Lawrence, the land is generally low but few hills of any considerable height, the soil is sandy with a mixture of clay, there is very little stone in this land upon the surface although the quarries of freestone appear commonly in the bed of the brooks. Considerable tracts of this land are very barren covered with a growth of small spruce. Many small pieces are covered chiefly with the beech, birch, and maple, and are good, but as much as half of this land is covered with a growth of spruce, fir, white birth and poplar mixed. This soil is a mixture of sand and clay. This would make a good land by being moderately manured, and will probably be much of it cultivated by the help of the great marshes of Cumberland and the intervals and wild meadow upon the streams between there and Pictou. I should think lime to be a good manure for this kind of land, as I have observed that it is always fertile where there is limestone in it. This sandy land will undoubtedly produce good hemp wherever it is, either naturally or by manure made rich enough to produce a good crop of any kind. Hemp has been raised on the interval of the River Philip and succeeded well. It appears that is only in the Eastern and Northeastern parts of the province that any considerable tracts of land can be found suitable for the culture of hemp. In the western part the old towns upon the Bay of Fundy, undoubtedly certain much land of a proper soil for hemp, but the back lands which were the immediate subject of my survey, contain but very little. The uncommonly good quality, as well as the great quantity of the marsh in the different parts of the head of the Bay of Fundy is undoubtedly owing to the unusual height and current of the tide waters. This current is sufficient to keep the water always muddy, and a portion of the finest part of the soil which is torn from the banks, or brought by brooks into the Bay is constantly deposited upon the marshes at spring tides. The soil of these marshes is usually a reddish loamy of nearly the same kind as is found in intervals upon fresh water rivers -- The height and steepness of the banks of the Parsborough shore seem to indicate that the water has gained upon the land considerably: the rocks there in places are of a kind which evidently decays, where it is exposed to the air, but I saw but few places where I had reason to think that the bank lost more than a foot annually upon an average. In travelling through the province I have observed with pleasure that the farmers in general appear to think themselves in a happy condition. In several places I have seen persons bringing up a large family of sober industrious children, whose habits of intemperance would probably have made them useless members of society if they had lived in a seaport, but the charm of acquiring property, constant employment, and above all the difficulty of procuring the means of gratifying their appetites in a new settled place, have got the better of habits, which in a different situation would have proved their ruin. I have in the course of my tour, met with many whose kindness has laid me under an obligation, but not a single person whom I have had any reason to complain of -- Many of our new settlers were originally tradesman, and most of those who were farmers had been accustomed to land which required a different mode of cultivation so that they are often necessarily somewhat awkward at their business. It is generally customary here in clearing new land to fall the trees every way as they happen to lean, the branches are cut off, and the body of the tree cut into lengths of about 12 feet: the bushes and logs are then made into piles and burnt. By the following method, which is at present much practised in the States of America, land is cleared with much less labour, and is in much better order for a crop. The trees should be all girdled by cutting out a single chip all round the tree, so as to cut through the bark or (which is a better method, have the bark stripped off for two or three feet in length, at the season when it parts easily from the tree. The trees are left in this condition for 5 or 6 years, by which time the small roots are nearly rotten: the branches of the trees decayed and the bodies of the trees are partly rotten below where they are girdled, so that they can be felled with very little labour. The underwood is then either cut or grubbed up and piled in heaps, after which the trees are cut down, care being taken to fall them parallel to each other, the branches break to pieces in falling the trees, and require very little chopping.

The logs are not cut but burnt into proper lengths by laying small piles of the dry branches across them, which are set on fire in dry weather, in the summer and require to be attended for 2 or 3 days to renew the fires, which after a small notch is burnt in the log only require a single dry stick across the log, as the bodies of the trees are very dry. After the trees are burnt into pieces they are drawn together by oxen and piled: they are much lighter than when fresh cut, and being dry burn with more ease. The land which is cleared in this manner is easily worked as the small roots are chiefly decayed. Trees may be girdled at any season of the year, but as they are much weakened by it, they often blow down, before the branches are sufficiently decayed to break to pieces, stripping off the bark is not attended with this inconvenience, but it can only be performed in the summer, which is as busy season with the farmer. The moose appear to be almost entirely destroyed in most parts of the province, the few which remain are chiefly in that of the province which lies west of La Have River--The Caribou are most numerous than the moose, but are very few compared to what they have been heretofore, owing to the fires, which have burnt over the open barrens and destroyed the white Reindeer moss which is their principal food. They herd together, and are most numberous upon the hills, south of Digby and the Annapolis River, and upon the mountains between West Chester and Pictou in the summer season, in the winter they usually approach the southern sea coast if the snow should be deep.

The beaver are almost all destroyed, although there is perhaps no country where they have been more numerous heretofore than in the barren part of this province, as appears from the remains of their old houses, canals etc. which are to be found upon almost every one of the innumerable small lakes in the rocky part of the province. I have not seen more than half a dozen inhabited beaver houses in the whole course of my tour. The consequence of this scarcity of game is that the internal parts of the province are but little frequented by the Indians in the winter. In the summer they take considerable quantities of salmon, gaspereus and eels, in the different rivers which they frequent. I think a considerable number of them have left the province, as I have been informed at many different settlements, that there are not half so many Indians about them as there was some years ago. Several of them are employed in the Fisheries in different places, and a small number as labourers by the farmers, but the greater part choose to follow their ancient mode of living, and make up the deficiency of their hunting by making baskets and other small articles (which they barter for provisions) and by begging. They are so much addicted to drinking and suffer so much from their own indolence that I think their number must be decreasing. I have been informed that the French government formerly allowed a small pension to such of the Acadians as married Indians but that these marriages did not produce the expected effect of making the Indians one people with the French.

The Frenchmen who married Indian women brought up their children to the same employed that they followed themselves: but the French women who married Indian men were obliged to become squaws, nor did the mixture of French blood seem to effect any change in the manners of their children, who possessed the same gravity and reserve as the other Indians. Notwithstanding the low condition to which the Indians are reduced they still retain a considerable portion of national pride and are many of them, much influenced by their religion: they are extremely indolent and immoderately addicted to intoxication, the consequence of which is that they often suffer extremely with hunger, yet I have never heard of an instance of a theft committed by any Indian who had not been very much accustomed to the company of white people. At Tusket there are usually a number of cattle which follow the rivers up for 20 miles above the settlements and remain there till fall among the Indians, who (though sometimes driven by hunger into the village) have never been suspected to have killed any of the cattle. I have been informed of several instances of Indians who came of their own accord and paid people for salmon, which they had taken out of their nets, sometime before, when it want [?]--At the close of the American war, a period when the game was much more numerous than it is now, the Indians had divided all hunting ground among their families, they did not kill more moose than was necessary to supply themselves with provisions as they considered them as their own property an Indian travelling through the hunting ground of another might kill any game he met with if he was in want of provisions, but he usually informed the proprietor of what he had done and offered him the skin, which the proprietor usually refused of this acknowledgement of his right. If an Indian found a trap set upon his land, he put a stone in it and sprung it, and if he found any Indians (not travelling) who were camped upon his land without his permission, he took away all the undried skins he found in their camp whilst they said not a word to oppose his right. Upon the great influx of inhabitants into the province after the American War many new settlements being formed and great numbers of moose killed by white hunters, the Indians in general seem to have resolved to destroy the game rather than share them with the Whites: in many places they killed ten times as many as they could make use of, and in the course of three or four winters almost entirely destroyed the moose and greatly diminished the Caribou.

The following names are taken from M. Bellin's map published in Charlevoix's <u>History of New France</u>.

French Names	Modern English Names
Emchie	Ramsheg
Tatamegouche	Tatmagouche
Antigoniche	Antigonish
Canceau	Canso
Paspebia	Petpiswick
Sincembre	Sambro
Mirligueche	Malagash
Port Kaltois	Port Midway
Port Mouton	Port Matson
Port aux Ours (Bear Harbour)	Port Hebert
Port Razoir	Port Roseway
Poboneau	Pubnico
Riviere Imbert	Bear River
Cap Chignitou	Cape Chignecto
Riviere de Pigiguit	Pisaquid River

I have been informed that the Indian syllable "Che" (which occurs in Chebucto, Chedebucto, Richibucto, Chepody, Chignecto, and many other proper names of places(signifies "great" as, Che-bucto, the Great Harbour.

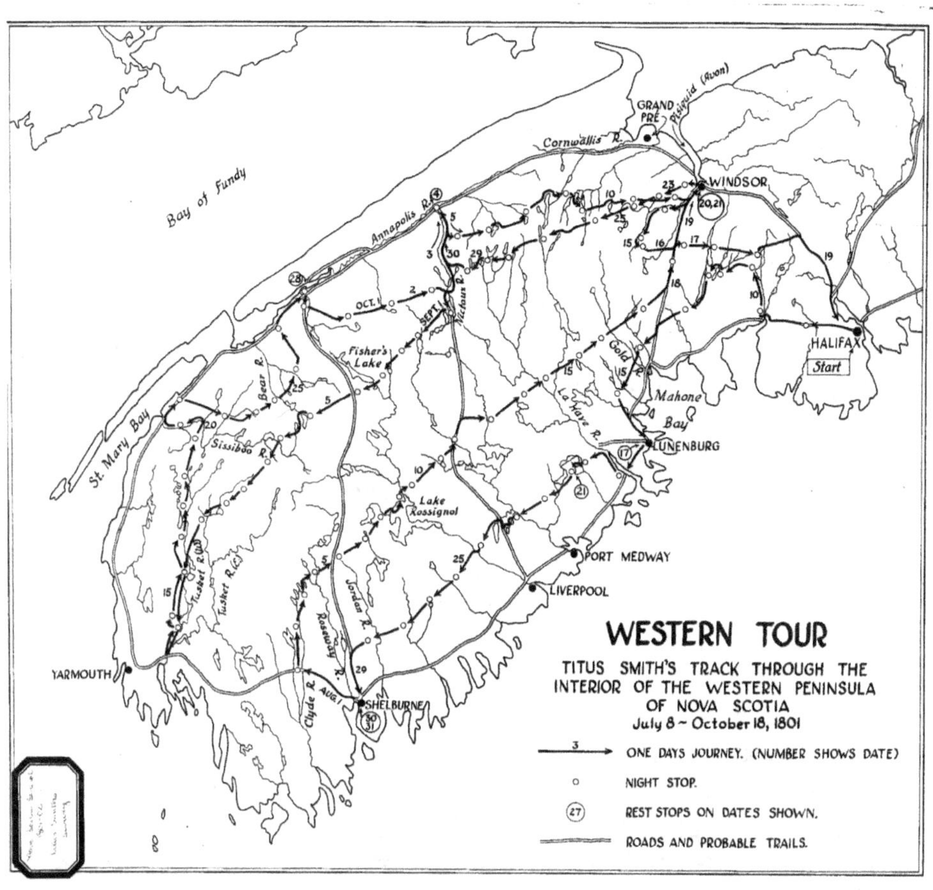

102 days
614 miles

THE WESTERN TOUR

<u>July 8th 1801.</u>

Left home at 12 o'clock and travelled towards Margarets Bay in the Foot-way which goes from the Dutch Village.

<u>9th.</u>   Arrived at the bay, proceeded to the Head of it and crossed the River which runs in there, then turned W. across the Head of the Bay for 1 mile and came to another River, went up it, Course N. 1 Mile. (These Rivers are each of them about the size of Big Salmon River in Preston) From the Dutch Village Boundary to within a Mile of Margarets Bay the Ground is chiefly a Solid Rock of the coarse millstone granite, scarce a single stone of any other kind to be seen; Part of the distance (perhaps 1/3) there is a little sand and Gravel, the Remainder has no soil but Turf, most of the ground has the Solid Rock covered some Depth with loose Stones. Within 6 miles of the bay are a Number of Lakes chiefly south of our path. Along the side of the Bay the Land is composed of sand and Gravel, apparently made by the decayed Granite, it is commonly very full of Rocks of the same Kind. It produces tolerable Crops when manured. The Points of Land which we saw on the other Side of the Bay are chiefly mountainous Hills of Granite. I was informed by several people here that the Hill of Achpotagen is a solid Rock of the same Kind; this, together with finding that it would occasion a considerable Delay prevented us from going there, as this Kind of Stone is all of the most unpromising for Minerals of any Kind, & there are besides, Hills above the Head of the Bay, apparently little inferior to this in Height which will not be much out of our Course.

<u>10th.</u> Proceeded 8 Miles N., halted at the N. end of a Lake belonging to the River by which we lay last Night. Land about half Sand & Gravel & very rocky, the other half all Rock, or loose Stones covered with Turf; Stones wholly the

coarse Granite - Hills very high and steep, the highest appear at Top to be solid Rocks, often so steep and ragged that it is impossible to climb them for some distance. For about 3 Miles from the bay The Timber has been destroyed by Fire; above that is chiefly Spruce, Hemlock, and pine with a very little hardwood in some places. there is a considerable Quantity of good building Timber & some spruce Spars but it would be almost impossible for Cattle to go upon great Part of this Ground except in winter. The Land is worst and most rocky in the last part of our Days walk. There are a great Number of Trees blown down, (in some Places for ¼ Mile all of them) which makes it difficult travelling.

11th. Went N. W. 3 miles - Land very hilly - some earth almost every where, but more of the Surface Rocks. The Tops of the Hills generally show the solid Rock - Timber Hemlock & tall Spruce, the Spruce seldom more than 16 Inches diameter, on the Tops of the highest Hills and Mixture of Beech - Here from the Top of a tall spruce I could see N. & N. E. about 8 miles, E. about 4 Miles. high Hills - Timber the same as above. - Marked the spruce and went W. for 1½ Miles, then W. S. 1½ Miles farther. Land about half tall Spruce from 6 to 16 Inches big, the other half scrubbed black Spruce Bushes; little or no Earth any where. The Parts covered with Bushes are nearly level except that the Surface is wholly composed of Rocks from 3 to 15 Feet diameter, where the Timber is large it is hilly, but very rough with Rocks. At the end of 4½ Miles we passed a small Brook running N. and ½ Mile farther a larger one running S. saw no other Brook or Lake this day. The Timber where we have traveled today is ¼ of it blown down, this, together with the Number of precipices we were obliged to avoid, make our progress very slow and difficult.

12th. Went S. 70 W. for ½ Mile & struck a Lake 3 Miles long its Course N. E. 7 S. W. Went about a Mile to its N. E. End, where a Brook about the Size of Tremains falls into it. Steered S. 70 W. again for 2 Miles & struck another

Lake, 1½ Miles from its N. End: we could see southerly 2 Miles but the Lake does not end there. Land for the last Mile Hardwood and Hemlock. Soil gravelly & rocky; the Remainder rough Hills of Rocks covered with tall Spruce - very little Earth on it - Remarkably delayed by windfalls being sometimes obliged to spend ½ hour in going 100 yards we halted about 3 o'clock an Account of Rain

13th. followed the Lake to the S. End with the view of seeing if it would not be of Use in carrying Timber to the Seacoast. It is about 5 Miles long, its general Course S. 25 W. except that for ½ Mile at the Head it turns westward, it has no Communication with the other Lake although it comes very near it. A Brook of no great Size falls into the southern end of it. On the East Side of the Lake a hardwood hill extends from where we struck the lake, two Miles to the Southward, the Remainder rocky spruce and Hemlock - om the W. Side rough Hills of Rock covered with small Spruce & White Birch till within 1½ M.S of the Head, where there is a Mixture of Hemlock & Hardwood. We followed the Brook W. for ½ M. when it turned N. of W. and we left it and continued our Course W. for 2 Miles on high Barrens covered with white Moss, small Spruce, Whortle & dwarf Laurel Bushes, - could see the Barrens 2 Miles S.

14th. Proceeded S. 60 W. 5 Miles; the first 2 Miles in this 2 Mile crossed a narrow Hwd hill rocky hills covered with fine Spruce Timber, then Barrens for 1 Mile; Large spruce for a Mile farther, when we came to hardwood & struck the Road, we found a Tree there marked A/30 when we had come a quarter Mile we followed it about a Mile to the Southward mostly on hardwood looking for Milemarks; not finding any, we resumed our Course and went 1 Mile on rough Barrens. We saw 4 or 5 small Lakes this Day with little Brooks running Southward. The Weather having been raining these 2 Days we were obliged to halt early to dry out Clothes. The Stones continue still wholly the coarse

Millstone Granite. Ever since we left the River of Mts. Bay we have frequently seen Caribou Tracks.

15th. Continued our Course S. 60 W. ½ Mile and struck a Lake about a Mile long: turned S. ½ Mile to avoid it. continued our Course S. 60 W for 8 Miles; within ½ Mile after we passed the Brook which runs out of the Lake, we struck Gold River - 4½ MS. farther the Middle River - the Land after we passed the first River has had the Timber destroyed by Fire, probably 30 or 40 years ago, and is covered with a young Growth. Land for 2 Miles after we passed Gold River, Beech & yellow Birth, soil gravelly & stoney, poor for Hardwood - from there to the middle River chiefly white Birch & Poplar with a Mixture of Spruce, very poor Soil after passing the middle River went up hill for 2 Ms. on rocky barrens covered with small Trees of black Spruce, white, & yellow Pine last Mile level, covered with white Birch & Poplar - between the two Rivers considerable Quantities of Slate & Mountain Stone - after passing the middle River wholly the coarse Granite.

16th. Turned S. and proceeded 6 Miles to Mushamush, took the Road from there to Lunenburg - Land the first 3 Miles chiefly rocky Barrens: the Remainder a poor Soil covered with a mixture of white Birch, Poplar, white & Yellow Pine, & Oak.

17th. employed in writing & in procuring Supplies. This District, which supplies the Halifax Markets with the greatest part of their Vegetables & Hay, has, in general, but a poor Soil naturally and has been brought to its present State of Cultivation, Solely by the uncommon Industry of the Inhabitants.

18th. Came to La Haive; Mr. Pernette did not think there were any Indians here that would be of Use to us, informed us of several Lakes on Petite Riviere but did not think either of them to be Lake Rossingnol. Mr. Pernette showed us a Specimen of a Kind of Iron Ore of which he informed us there was plenty, & which he had assayed, it yielded about ¼ its Weight of Iron. It is not a pure Ore but contains a great deal of Slate cemented together with it. We observed that the Swamps were covered with very irony Water & that the Slate, of which there is abundance here, contains much of the Sulphurous Iron Pyrites.

<u>19th.</u> Left Mr. Pernettes and went about 7 Miles up the river there followed a road W. for 2½ Miles to a Saw Mill on a Branch of Petit Riviere where we lay. Went to see one Mohlman who came through from Annapolis with Mr. Wheelock, he says that the Nictaw & La Have Rivers do not head in the same Lake, but that a Lake on the one comes within 1½ Mi. Of a Lake on the other. He says that the large Lake of La Haive has 2 Rivers fall into it, one of which heads near Mushamush and the other he is informed by Indians extends almost to Annapolis -- the La Haive is navigable for Vessels of 400 Tons, for 16 Miles up, as I am told, (it extends 18 Miles to the Falls) but it has a Bar at the Entrance which has not more than 18 Feet of Water at low Tides. The Soil is generally poor and stoney next the Water, it is something better ½ Mile back where there is Hardwood in some places - in general the Land is or has been covered with Spruce & Hemlock.

<u>20th.</u> Went S. W. 4 Miles. Course & Distance uncertain, as we attempted to follow the Lake, & were so hemmed by this Labyrinth of Water that after going three Miles we found ourselves within ½ Mile of the Place we set off from. Towards Night we made a Shift to reach some high Land where I endeavoured by climbing Trees to get some Idea of the Place we had been so puzzled by. There is a flat Barren, perhaps 3 Miles broad which stretches from the Mill for 6 or 8 Miles a Course S. of W. a Lake, or rather a Number of Lakes reach through this Barren, from just above the Mill a Lake reaches 1 ½ Miles then, for 1 Mile farther several little Lakes separated by Bars of Rock which the water falls

over; the Remainder a Single Lake. These Lakes, especially the last are full of Islands, & composed of long Coves branching from each other so that it is almost impossible to go ½ Mile any way on the Barren without striking some Branch of them. We were informed that a little below the Mill there is a Lake 4 Miles long on the same Brook. The Barren is nearly ½ mossy Swamp covered with small Bushes & Black spruce Poles; the Remainder broken Rocks of blue Mountain Stone with a thicket of small Bushes, & in many Places yellow Pine about 1 Foot Diameter at Right we steered S. for ½ Mile to a H.wood hill.

<u>21st</u>.   Being sick in the Morning did not move till after Noon we proceeded S. 55 W. for ½ Mile and struck the Lake again; could see a point of it at about 3 Ms. distance bearing S. 20 W. being too faint to travel, halted again.

<u>22nd</u>. Followed the Lake to a distance of 3 Ms. S. 20 W., & ¾ of Ml. W., there is a Hwood hill of no great Breadth, but of a good quality in the places marked H Wood: the Bottom of the Hill next the Lake is very rocky, covered with Spruce & Hemlock, the Islands in the Lake all Barrens. Left the Lake at o & steered S. 70 W., ¾ Ml. mostly on hardwood, & struck a Lake 1 Mile long lying N. W. & S. E., set of ½ Ml. N. W. to avoid it & proceeded S. 70 W. 4 Miles upon Land which has no Hill more than 10 Feet higher than the Vallies - The first 2 miles ½ Spruce Swamps chiefly too low & mossy for wild Grass; the other half rough rocky Barrens - the last 2 Ms. poor, stoney Land covered with Pine from 18 to 30 Inches diameter at the Butt, in general with a Mixture of Oak, white Birch & Beech. A considerable Number of Spars might be cut here which would run from 60 to 70 Feet, but far the Largest Part are too crooked, & many are too short for Most Timber. The small Trees are in general nearly equal in Height to the large ones - some of the Trees are yellow Pine, but more than 3/4s are white Pine. Passed a Brook about the Size of Freshwater R. course S. within ½

Ml. of where we halted; saw no other Brook this day except 2 or 3 very small Rivulets.

23rd. Proceeded S. 55 W. 4 Miles; halted about 2 o'clock, as it rained ever since Sunrise. Land for the first 3 Miles 1/3 Swamps, the Remainder very rough with Rocks, covered with a Thicket of small Spruce & Fir, with Pines at the Distance of 5 or 6 Rods from each other some of which would be useful for Boards, but none of them for Mast Timber. the last 2 Miles less rocky, covered chiefly with Pine from 3 Feet to 18 Inches Big at Butt. Numbers which will answer for Masts. but very few which will run more than 60 Feet. within 2 Miles of where we halted passed a Brook, Course S. E. about the Size of fresh water R. Within 1 Mile of where we halted passed a River about 6 Rods broad & waist-deep supposed to belong to Port Midway - no Interval upon it - very fine Pines near it. These Two Days past we have seen some Moose Tracks and have hardly ever been out of Sight of fresh Caribou Tracks. No Hills of any considerable Height this Day except 2 or 3 Heaps of Rocks about 40 Feet high. Rocks the blue Mountain Stone.

24th. proceeded S. 55 W. 6 Miles at the End of ¼ Ml. struck a Lake about ¾ Ml. across, went round it into our course.   a Mile farther struck another of an irregular Shape which continued at our Right for a Mile; it might be 2 Miles from N. to S. Both Lakes are shallow Rocks above Water in many places, and are nearly surrounded by low Barrens. At the End of 4 Miles we struck the Liverpool Road, Marked some Trees & went a little to the S. in the Road & found a Tree badly marked which appeared to be intended for XVM. A Mile farther on our course struck a Brook about the Size of Tremains, supposed to belong to Liverpool R. were very much delayed by it as we struck it in a large Marsh where it was a deep River, the Water being raised by the Rain yesterday and we were obliged to go a long way up to avoid the Marsh & some burnt land where all the Trees had fallen down. Land till we came to L1. Rr. ½ Hemlock very stoney, the Remainder Spruce Swamps & Thickets - Pine in some places, too short for Mast Timber - the Marsh contains above 100 Acres ¼ of which is good for wild Grass, the Remainder mossy. Barrens about it - At Night came to a very rocky Hill covered with Pine, Oak, white Birch & Poplar. Observed the Report of Cannon, supposed to be at Liverpool, to bear S. 40 E.

25th. proceeded S. 55 W. a mile & struck Liverpool River, went up it 1 Mile a little W. of N. and came to rapid Falls, but were not able to ford it, it being greatly swelled by the late Rain. Made a Raft & crossed it, and proceeded S. 70 W. for 3 Miles. Land till we came to the River covered with large Rocks, with a growth of small Pine, white Birch & poplar near the River some large short pines & Oaks. Along the River there is about 20 Rods breadth of March, part of which might produce a tolerable Crop of wild Grass. After passing the River went up a rocky Hemlock Hill & came upon a flat, spruce Barren which has been burnt last summer.

26th. Rained hard at daylight, made a Camp & lay still as the burnt Land would not shelter us from either wind or Rain, and we did not expect if we advanced to be able to procure Materials to make a Camp, which we had near us by chance - the Rain stopping towards Night we proceeded S. 70 W. 2½ Ms. flat burnt Land ¾ Me. - the Remainder 3 naked, level Mossbogs which have no Wood on them, and appear to have been originally shallow Lakes - we sink on them now about 1 Foot in Water.

27th. proceeded S. 65 W. 10 MS., at the End of 1 Mile touched the N. End of a small Lake, 1 Mile farther crossed a Brook the Size of Fresh Water Rr.; 1 Mile farther another; same Size; at the End of 9 Miles a third, same Size, Course of all Southward. Land the first 5 Miles a level Swamp, with Islands of upland which occupy 1/3 of it; about 1/3 naked moss Bogs - could see on some of them 4 Miles N. & 2 Ms. S. all burnt over except Mossbogs - the last 5 Miles something more than ½ Swamps, the Remainder burnt spruce Land - Soil of the Upland where it is not covered with Rocks, Sand & Gravel - Rocks always the blue mountain Stone. several of the last Swamps we passed are not burnt, and are haunted by Moose, the Brook first mentioned we were obliged to go up ¾ of a Mile to pass it - saw in that Space about 50 acres of good wild Meadow on it, which continued farther up & farther down, - saw in several other places small pieces (seldom larger than 2 or 3 Acres) of good Meadow - besides the Brooks above mentioned we passed innumerable small Rivulets, & the Swamps are mostly mid-leg deep in Water which all runs S. Saw no Hill this Day more than 10 Feet higher than the Swamp next it - saw no H. Wood except some soft Maple on the Brooks.

28th. Proceeded S. 65 W. 5 Miles and struck Jordan River. Were obliged to make a Raft to pass it, on Account of the Freshet. After passing it went S. 60 W. 2 Ms. Land to the River about half Swamps - the first 3 Ms. went down Hill a little - The Upland not so stoney but that it might be cultivated were the soil good - it is however exceedingly poor and barren, covered with small black Spruce. The Swamps chiefly covered with spruce, did not see more than 1500 Acres of naked Moss Bogs this Day. The last 4 Miles Land Hilly - Hills the same Soil as at Mushamush, a Mixture of Sand & Gravel composed partly of decayed Granite, which here begins to appear again, tho' the Porphyry still continues. This has been burnt formerly as well as last year, the Swamps excepted. It has been covered on the Hill with Pine & white Birch mixed with Fir & Spruce - the Vallies all Spruce, either mossy Swamps, or Beds of Rock. This Soil is too poor for Cultivation where manure cannot be procured from the Seashore unless where Meadows could be found which might enable the Farmer to keep a Number of Cattle.

29th. Continued our Course S. 60 W. for three Miles & struck the Annapolis Road about 13 Miles from Shelburne, followed it to Town on Land the same as last described

except that it grows more stoney near the Town. The Soil &
Rocks full of Ising-glass. The Land which has been manured
produces very good Crops; it is a warm Soil which brings
every thing forward fast & it must be more secure against
Drought than the manured Land near Halifax, as the Soil, like
all sandy Land, is so loose as to enable the Roots to strike
deep. This Town possesses a Mineral Spring which has I as I
am informed by Numbers of People effected several Cures of
old Sores particularly sore Legs of some years standing. It is
in the Edge of a Brook in a Piece of Marshy Ground, but a
Wall has been built about it which prevents the Brook Water
from mixing with it. It has a strong sulphureous or
bilgewater Smell and Taste; it has likewise a saline Taste I
was not able to procure any Galls to try it with, but thought I
could perceive the Taste of Copperas & Epsom Salt. The
Stones about if have nothing uncommon in them, & the
Spring boils up from the Bottom, and probably from a
considerable Depth. This Water frequently bursts bottles
when they are close corked.

30th & 31st. Employed in writing & providing for the
Woods.

August 1st.   Proceeded on the Road to Yarmouth as
far as Mr. James Hamiltons 12 Miles from Shelburne, & 1½
Miles beyond Cape Negro River. As he is a Surveyor & better
acquainted with the woods here than any other Person about
Shelburne, we were very glad to meet with him, as we found
that Mr. Robinson was at Halifax at the time we arrived at
Shelburne, Mr. Hamilton with the utmost Readiness gave us
all the Information in his Power. He said that we should not
find a Foot of good Land between his House & Argyle, the
greatest part of the Land towards Barrington & Argyle was
covered with Rocks, & the Remainder like the Land near his
House which is a poor Sand covered in general with Pine,
some spots, a little better with a Mixture of white Birch Oak
& poplar. He told us that the Cape Negro River bears E. of
N. from his house which is nearly N. W. from Shelburne. He

showed us an Indian Plan of the River for about 20 Miles above him containing a great Number of Lakes which occupy 1/3 of the Land, he directed us to as the Course we had best follow, to find our Way among them, for in Consequence of Information received from Him we resolved not to go to Argyle but to go up Cape Negro River till we were far enough N. and then steer for Falmouth. He said that in going up the River we should see the best Land near him as it would grow much more rocky & barren is we turned E. or W. - he says that after passing Yarmouth in going towards Sissiboo the Stones change to another Kind & the soil alters for the Better - that there is considerable H.woods high up some of the Branches of the Tusket River. Mr. Hamilton notwithstanding the Poverty of this Soil has the best Crop on his Land that I have seen near Shelburne, altho he has settled 12 Miles from any other Inhabitants, but he has the advantage of a Meadow which enables him to keep a large Stock of Cattle & his Family appear to be uncommonly ingenious as well as industrious, which enables them to live without the Help of others much better than Persons would who could not like him do all their own Work themselves. N. B. Many of the Hills near Shelburne would produce good Pine were it not that Fires are so frequent that it does not get Time to grow.

<u>2d.</u>   Left the Road about 1 Mile W. of Cap Neg. R. & proceeded N. 10 E. for 6 Miles - Land partly spruce Swamps, partly sandy Hills covered with Spruce, white Birch, Poplar, Oak & Pine & a Few places with large yellow Birch, the first we have seen on this side Liverpool River. There is a Thicket of small Fir almost every where on the Upland among the large Trees - Spruce large enough for building Timber. As from the information we received there is Reason to expect very bad Travelling, resolved to live upon 3 Biscuit per day each, & to endeavour to procure Game for the Remainder.

<u>3d.</u>   Proceeded N. 10 E. 5 Miles. At the End of 1½ Miles passed a Brook about the Size of Sackville River, 1½ Ms. farther another size of Tremains; at the lower End of a

Lake a Mile long, - considerably delayed by each of them –
Land 2/3 Spruce Swamps & low Spruce Barrens - the
Remainder Rocky Hills covered with Hemlock, Spruce, & pine
-- N. B. the first Hemlock we had seen since we were a Mile
this side of Liverpool River.

The low Ground so thick set with Bushes & 3 Feet high, in
many places, that it is as tiresome & difficult to travel
through as if it was deep covered with Snow –

    <u>4th.</u>   Proceeded N. 10 E. for 3 Miles - At the End of 1
Mile passed a Brook, size of Tremains, Course S. E. at the
Head of a Lake a Mile long - saw another Lake on each Side
of this nearly parrallel to it - Sandy rocky Hills between the
Lakes covered with white Birch, Oak & Poplar. last 2 Miles
went up Hill on Barrens covered with scrubbed Pine & black
Spruce; the Ground covered with the white Reindeer Moss &
Arbutus [? acadiensis.] Turned N. 65 E. and proceeded 4
Miles to Cape Negro R. all the way upon Barrens & Swamps,
the last 2 Miles has been burnt over ten or twelve years ago,
& the Timber has great part fallen down. luckily there near
was much growing on the dry parts - Ever since we Left Mr.
Hamiltons we have seen abundance of Tracks of Moose &
Bear till we came to the burnt Land, being probably driven
into this Piece of green Woods by the Fires last Summer,
within ¼ Mile after we changed our Course passed a Brook,
size of Tremains, 2 Miles farther another same Size. Course
Southerly.

    <u>5th.</u>   Proceeded N. 65 E. for 5 Miles. - the first 4
Miles burnt Barrens covered with large Rocks, (from 10 to 20
Feet diameter) almost impassable in many Places on Account
of the old Growth of Wood's lying on the Ground - no young
Growth of Trees, altho' burnt long ago - covered with dwarf
Laurel, [? Whortle] & Blueberry Bushes, sweet Farm & other
small shrubs. the [? barrenest] Hills with acadian Arbutus &
some small kind of [Heath.] Last Mile not burnt, chiefly
swamps; several small, very steep, and pretty high Hills, the

sides covered with Pine, the Tops with Oak, white Birch & poplar - the highest Hills which we saw has 20 Acres on the Top whose Timber is 1/3 Beech of a small size.

    <u>6th</u>.   Proceeded N. 65 E. 6 Miles: At the End of 1 Mile passed a Brook, Size of Tns., Course S., about 1 Mile below a Lake which it runs from: At the End of 4 Ms. struck a Lake which we made a Raft to pass, altho' it was not More than ¾ Mile to the Southern End of it, but it has cost us more than an Hour to go ¼ Mile before we struck it, the Timber being almost all burnt down near it. the N. End of the Lake we could not see as it turned eastward. At Night struck a Lake about 1 Mile broad at the S. End narrower at the N. & turns westward out of Sight - Land for 2 Miles spruce Swamps & rocky Hills covered with Pine, spruce, & small Hemlock, then for 2 Ms. burnt Barren covered with small black Spruce - last 2 Miles steep, rocky Hills covered with small Spruce & Hemlock, a few H.wood Trees on their summits - where we halted about 40 Acres covered with small Beech, - could see on the N. W. side of the Lake a naked Barren covered with large Rocks. From the Shape of the Land I should think the two Lakes to be only 2 different parts of the same Lake.

    <u>7th</u>.   Continued N. 65 E. 3 Miles when we struck a River about the Size of big Salmon River; as it runs very gently here, it is deep so that we could not ford it - spent the Remainder of the Day in making a Raft and mending our Clothes. Land 1/3 Swamps some of which are good for wild Grass, the Remainder small rocky Hills covered with Spruce & Hemlock, 1 Foot diameter & less - about half burnt last Summer, which delayed & fatigued us very much, as the greater Part of the Trees are fallen down where they are so large. Observed that the Lake continues to farther to the N. E. than we had seen before.

    <u>8th</u>.   Passed the River & continued our Course N. 65 E. for 2 Miles when we struck a very large Lake - Land but little higher than the River & Lake - about ½ swamp, the

Remainder covered with Rocks, from where we passed the River to where it empties into the Lake there is generally about 12 Rods breadth of good wild Meadow covered with blue joint Grass, farther from the River the marsh grows worse - As this is the largest Lake we have seen suppose it to be Lake Rossignol we attempted to follow the Shore but found it would be impracticable to go so far as to see much of the Lake with our Stock of Provisions, so we could procure no Kind of Game. The Shore for some Miles being very low with many Marshes running into the Land which have always an impassable Creek in the Middle, the Marshes even where there is a large blue joint is covered from one to 2 Feet with water, the Land on their Edges either thickets of small Bushes growing among Rocks or burnt Land with the trees chiefly fallen; we therefore made a Raft on which we went 3 Miles on our Course, there being a fresh Breeze, which fortunately was fair. At the Place marked Hill on the N. E. side of the Lake there is a Hill covered with Hemlock, containing perhaps 100 Acres, which rises I should think 30 Feet above the Level of the Lake; there is also a small Swell on the S. E. side, & some small hills near where the River comes in; every where else the Land is very low, no Hills to be seen any way - the Middle of the Lake is not deeper than the Parts near the shore, for Rocks & small Islands are to be seen every way, & we hung frequently upon covered Rocks when more than a Mile from Land, whilst we could not reach Bottom at the other End of the Raft with poles 12 feet long. This Lake is not a regular valley filled with water, Like the Lakes in hilly Land, but a small concavity in a great Plain of Rocks, in which there are no proper Hills but only an unequal surface, which makes the shore so irregular that in many Places, by following the Lake one would go 10 Miles to reach a point which was not more than 2 distant from him - we have seen about 150 Acres of good wild Meadow on the River and Lake, perhaps 300 or poor which might be worth mowing; there must be more back, but that which lies off from the Lake is chiefly bad.   of upland we have seen about 100 Acres in different Pieces, mixed H. Wood & Hemlock &

the Remainder I should judge from the rocky Shore & from the exact Resemblance of the Timber to that of the Parts we were upon, to be a Bed of Rocks - The Stones which from Shelburne to where we lay last Night have been chiefly the coarse Granite with a small mixture of the blue mountain Stone, this Day wholly the Latter. Camped at Night on an Island in the Lake.

<u>9th</u>.   Continued our Course N. 65 E. for 1½ Miles to Land, proceeded 2 Ms. By Land and struck a Lake; were obliged to turn E for 1 Mile - near this Lake 2 Hills of Earth covered with Hemlock & white Birch, the first Hills or Earth we had seen since we left L. Ri. the Remainder being a Bed of large broken Rocks covered with small Pine & whortle Bushes, many places only covered with Moss; from the western Part of the Lake a Brook about the Size of freshwater R. runs southward, but is lost in the Rocks after running a few Rods.

<u>10th</u>. Continued the same Course for 6 Miles. First 1½ Ms, high Hemlock Hills with Vallies of rock between them; from a Tree on one of them could see high hills for 3 Ms., W. & N. W. covered with hemlock, Soil Sand & Gravel. Remaining 4½ Ms. covered with Rocks with a small Growth of white Birch, & a thick undergrowth of black whortle Bushes except the last ½ Ml, a sandy Hill covered with Poplar & small Oak, chiefly. At the End of 1½ Ms, passed a Brook running N., Size of Freshwater R. - in the Hemlock Land observed a very old Indian blazed Path, & some Foot paths.

<u>11th</u>. Continued our Course for 1½ Miles on stoney white Birch Land & struck the Liverpool Road 22 Ms. from Liverpool, followed the Road 3 Miles N. to Mr. Burks at Port Medway River, Land growing better as we proceeded. Timber a young Growth of white & yellow Birch, Beech, soft & hard Maple, Ash & Hornbeam, - very tall as the Road follows a Ridge we cannot judge of the Proportion of bad Land. Were informed by Mr. Burk that this Kind of Land

continues 8 Miles Northward along the Road when it grows barren till within 16 Miles of Nictau that the Nictau crosses the Road within 20 Miles of Annapolis River, coming from the Westward, 2 Miles this side of where the Nictau crosses the Road, a Branch of P. Medway crosses the Road coming also from the Westward, that on this River we are upon there is a Lake 8 Miles long 2 broad beginning 2 Miles from the Road, that parrallel to this, & in some places within ¾ Ml. of it lies another 10 Miles long & 4 broad in some places, bearing E. S. E., which receives the Branch of Port [? M. R.] mentioned above to cross the Road near where the Nictau does, it runs in & runs out near its W. End; * a Mistake. Wild Cat R. does not strike the great Le. But empties into P.M.R. above the Lake on that this great Lake has a great Tract of hardwood Land on the Northern Side, which is rocky, otherwise good. The large Lake on the Main Branch of P. M. R. has but poor Land about it. At the lower End of it is a Piece of Interval containing about 30 Acres called the Indian Gardens which has formerly been cultivated by the Indians, it has a large Cross standing on it, & a Number of Indian Graves. Between here & the Lake (a distance of 2 Ms.) lies a Piece of Interval containing 150 Acres, - Soil not extraordinary - no Elm upon it, - We learn here that the Li. Rr. Runs out of the large Lake which we passed. I think that Jordan Rr. Must run out of it also as the River which runs into it is as large as either of them & it must receive many small Streams; a great Allowance however must be made for Evaporation in such a large shallow Lake. 2 Miles before we came to Mr. Bs. We passed a Stream running east into P. M. R. larger than Trems. which I suppose receives the brooks which we passed running N. Mr. B. has been told by Indians that there is good Land reaching 20 Miles farther up P.M.R.

12th. Proceeded N. 4 Ms. along the Road and then turned Eastward for 3 Miles in a Footpath which goes to a Settlement begun by some young Men - Land ¾ fit for Cultivation, but as the best Land, is the best place for a Road we cannot judge the proportion -- there is here a very fine Meadow covered with blue joint Grass, supposed to contain 200 Acres or more. Mr. Burk has been informed by Indians that the Trees were all blown down he[re] by a Hurricane about 80 years ago, which was followed by a Fire the next year, after which the young Growth which now covers the Ground, came up. I am inclined to believe this Account from observing that there are considerable Tracts now covered with Beech, hard Maple, white Ash & Hornbeam, with so good a Soil that I think it never could have had much soft Wood on it, and consequently it could not have had the Timber destroyed by Fire only; yet it has not a single tree of the old Growth remaining on it.

    <u>13th</u>. Proceeded N. 67 E. for 8 Miles. first 1½ Miles Hills covered with young hard wood & small Swamps very good for wild Grass. Then for 2 Ms. a level Barren of Slate, generally solid & not covered with loose Stones. Then for 3½ level stoney Land, covered with young H.wood, being the same Slate Rock with a shallow Soil it is perhaps 1 Mile of moist Ground in several pieces which would produce good Grass, the Remainder dry & poor. Last mile hilly, and good, except that it is so stoney as considerably to impede Cultivation - At the End of 1 Mile passed a Brook larger that Tms. - at the End of 5 Ms. another, size of Fresh W. R. - where we halted a third rather larger than Tms. Courses of all S. this last runs into a Lake within 40 Rods of which awe can see near 2 Ms. S. E. it there turns Eastward out of Sight.

    <u>14th</u>. Proceeded N. 67 E. for 7 Miles - Land chiefly covered with Slate, with the young Growth of Timber continuing. passed in different Hills about 2 Miles of pretty good Land which I think to have been formerly Hardwood. about 2 Ms. of poor very stoney Land, & 3 of a Kind of Barren (nearly level) covered now with scrub white Birth, Oak & Spruce but which we see had originally a Growth of large Pine on it as the Trees are not yet entirely decayed. very little Earth here; almost wholly Slate Stones. At the End of 4 Miles passed 2 small Rivulets running N. neither of them ½

the Size of Freshwater Rr.; ½ Mile farther struck Mr. Wheelocks Road, 1 Mile after passing this struck La Have River, which is here about 6 Rods broad & 1 Foot deep. It lies in a great Valley between 2 Hills higher than Halifax Hill. there is a considerable breath of flat Ground in the Valley, but not more than 20 Rods Breadth of Interval (for 1 Mile the distance we examined), the Remainder being a Bed of Slate Rocks. The Soil of the Interval is inferior to that of the Intervals to the Eastward, but it has a little Elm upon it, the first we have seen on this side of Halifax. At the Top of the Hill on the W. side of the River is about ½ Miles Breadth of good Land. Ever since we passed Cape Negro River, the Eastern side of every Hill we have passed has invariably been the best Land –

15th. Continued N. 67 E. for 6 Miles, set off ½ more to the N. W. than we did to the S. E.- Land hilly - first 4 Ms. ½ good Upland, ½ poor stony upland, & Swamps which are very good for Timothy Grass. Next Mile chiefly an Alder Swamp, in which there is not enough adventitious Soil to cover the Rocks, but which I think would bear Timothy Grass, as it is very full of Blackberries, Virgins Bower, Touch me not; & other Plants of rich Land. - Last Mile a Spruce Barren, a solid, unbroken Rock of the Blue Mountain Stone; the first very bad place for a Road we have seen since we left the Li Road. At the End of 3 Miles struck a Brook about the Size of Sackville R. which we supposed to be the other Branch of La Haive, its Course S. W.; we followed it up more than a Mile but found no Interval - the best Hills of Upland we passed were by the sides of it, some Elm upon them & a great Deal of Cohosh Spikenard & other Interval Plants   the young Growth of Wood still continues - 1 Mile after we left the River struck a Lake more than a Mile long, with a small Brook running towards the River.

16th. Continued N. 67 E. for 7 Ms. first Mile Barrens in which the Rock changes to the coarse millstone Granit. - then for 3 Ms. poor gravelly Land covered chiefly with poplar, except some small Spots on the Top of some of the Hills which bear Beech, & about ¼ Mile of very good Swamp - Last 3 Miles mountainous Barrens of Granite, with small Spots of Gravel here & there among the Rocks - Timber Black Spruce, white Birch, & Poplar. - 2 Ms. before we halted, could see from a high Rock high Land at a great Distance, supposed Achpotagoen, bearing S. 60 E. - from that point, by the East round to N. could see 10 Miles - Lofty Hills - general Colour that of Spruce - at the End of 1 Ml. passed the N. End of a Lake a Ml. long, just at Night touched another which appeared to be 2 Ms. long.

   17th   Proceeded the same Course for 8 Ms. - At the End of 2 Ms. crossed the Middle River of Chester, here about the Size Little Salmon R.   At the End of 6 Ms passed a Brook - size of Tms. Course W. of S Land all Barren, except 1½ Ml. before we came to the Brook last mentioned, where we travelled on a Hill by the [?] of the Brook, poor gravelly Soil, not very stoney, which had one been [?] large Pine, now with white Birch & Poplar 5 & 6 Inches big (a larger Size than what grows on the Barrens) with an Undergrowth of Dwarf Laurel & Whortle. After passing the Brook we came upon the Old Growth of Timber - for these last 3 Days we have been much impeded by Windfall, blown down in the great Storm, of which we had not seen any considerable Quantity before from the Time we left Lunenburg. The fallen Trees we met with Westward being burnt loose at the Roots.

   18th. Continued our Course N. 67 E. for 5 Ms. and struck the Chester Road 16 Ms. from Windsor. Land for 1 Ml. poor & stoney covered with Fir & Spruce 1 Foot big & under, then for ½ Ml. a hardwood Hill, (we had been constantly rising from Chester River to this hill, but going down small Hills and up larger; & had descended in the same Manner from the high Rock to the River) after going down this hill came upon Land more level than we had travelled for some Time - Timber for 1 M the same as in the Morning - then a Bed of Rocks covered with small black Spruce to the road and for 1 M in the Road, for 3 Miles farther not so stoney, covered with good spruce timber. Stones still continue the coarse Granite.

19th. Reached Windsor late, the Road being almost wholly obstructed by Windfalls - Land hilly, very full of Granite Rocks, till we descend into the Valley of Windsor. Timber great Part tall Spruce. Some small Tracts of hardwood, & larger of Barren hills, which are almost wholly Rocks. Where we first came into the Valley (I call it a Valley because it is surrounded by lofty Hills which almost wholly screen it from Winds) of Windsor or Falmouth, the Upland is free from Stone but poor & sandy, except where it has been enriched by Manure; after coming a little down the River the Soil is considerably mixed with Clay, as it is always near Plaster, which beings here. There are also large Quarries of Limestone here of the same Kind which I have seen on the Banks of Musquedoboit adjoining the Plaster; I observe that some parts of this Limestone decay into a kind of Marl of a dark chocolate Colour, which I think has given the Colour and Consistence of reddish Clay to the Soil of the Quince Trees bearing well here, and am told that Peaches grow well also. about 16 Bushels to the Acre is as I am informed the Average Crop of Wheat.

20th & 21st. Employed in providing Necessaries.

22nd. Set out late from Davisons Mill in Falmouth, about 3 Miles Nw. of Windsor River and went 4 Ms S. 70 W. Soil a mixture of Loam & sand in various Proportions. Last Mile very rocky - Stone the coarse Granite. Some small Swamps which are very good, - the Upland chiefly a good Soil to lay Manure upon, but not good enough to produce any considerable Crops without it, a few small pieces excepted, Timber white Birch & Poplar.

23d. Proceeded S. 80 W for 4 Miles, were obliged to halt by hard Rain, our Knapsacks being too heavy to travel in it. Land high Hills. ¾ of the surface covered either by loose Rocks or by swells of the solid Rock which forms the Hills - Timber; white Birch Poplar & Spruce. halted at Night by a Brook rather larger than Tremains; Course S.

24th. Proceeded S. 80 W. 6 Ms. at the End of the 1½ Ms. struck a Brook running E., which we followed up for ½ Ml. when the Course it came from changed to S. probably the same we left this Morning - Land - for 1 Mile Marsh, good for wild Grass, most of it on the Brook. about ½ Mile in two separate Pieces good Upland covered with yellow Birch & hard Maple; ½ Ml. in different Ash Swamps, good for English Grass; the Remainder almost wholly covered with Rocks, passed a Piece of 1 Acre which covered with the old Growth of Timber, all the Rest white Birch, Poplar & Spruce, which reaches some MS. N.

25th. Continued our Course for 5 Miles - first 2 Miles a thicket of Alder, of which 1/3 is good for wild Grass, the Remainder of Bed of large loose Rocks, which have a small quantity of rich Mud between them - This Land would bear Grass but could not be mowed. last 3 Ms. White Birch & spruce, nearly one half the Ground covered with Rocks, the Remainder a gravelly Soil. At the End of 2 Ms. crossed a Brook running N. size of Tns., 1 Ml. farther struck a Lake which lay athwart our Course 1½ Ms. long. the Brook above mentioned runs from its S. E. end, on the western side of this Lake lies a narrow Hill, a Mile long covered with yellow Birch & Maple. just at Night struck a small Lake not more than ¾ Ml. long.

26th. Continued S. 80 W. for 6 Ms. 1st 1½ Ml. ½ Alder Swamps, ½ white Birch upon chiefly covered with Rocks; then for 2 Ms. black Spruce Barrens of which about ½ is Swamp; then for ½ Mile a Hill covered with a Mixture of Beech, yellow Birch, Fir & Spruce, pretty stoney, but might be cultivated, next for 1 Mile a very barren thicket of Black Spruce & yellow Pine; last Ml. a Mixture of Beech, Birch, &

Fir. At the End of one Mile passed 2 Brooks, Size of F. W., Course N. one Mile before we halted passed another rather less, running N. it had where we passed it about 20 Acres of Alder Swamp. have seen this Day about 100 Acres which would make wild Meadows - Hills these [? 2] Days very small, could not get any distant Prospect from high Trees except back on our Course - Our Course for these last 3 Days must be very uncertain as the Swamps are so thick that we cannot see 20 Feet, & on the Upland our Way is almost always obstructed by Windfalls so that we are obliged to go on a very serpentine Line to find the easiest place to get through them.

27th. Continued our Course for 1 Mile & struck a Lake 1½ MS. long this with a broad miry Brook turned us near a Mile S.; Brook Size of Tns. running S. continued our course for 6 MS. At the End of 4 Miles passed a Brook Size of F. W. R. at the End of 5 Ms. another, same Size both running S. - timber this Day chiefly an old Growth, the first we have seen since we left Falmouth, a few Trees excepted; Land the 1st Mile hardwood, a good soil, then for 1 Mile Spruce Swamps & Barrens, then came upon hilly, very rocky Land, covered with Spruce mostly of which a considerable part is fit for building Timber, many small Spots less rocky, with a Mixture of Beech, Birch & hard Maple - At the End of 3 Ms. could see from the Top of a Tree 6 Ms. from S. W. to N. W. Land very hilly, ¼ hardwood, perceived that our Course would go through Spruce land chiefly. A large Valley extending a long way Southward in which are 2 Brooks last mentioned - saw very frequently this Day very old blazed Paths of the Indians. heard some Guns near & saw the Tracks of Indians, but did not find their Camp. Moose Tracks are frequent here & there have been great many Martin Traps 30 or 40 years ago.

28th. Continued S. 80 W. for 6 Ms. - Land for 4 Ms. chiefly covered with large Spruce & Hemlock - some small Pieces mixed with hard Wood. the soil of this good, but the Ground half covered by large Rocks. Last 2 Ms. Barrens

Timber black Spruce & small Pine; as much as 2/3 blown
down - At the End of 2 Ms. passed a brook, Size of F. W. - 2
Ms. farther another, same size. Course of both Southward.
At Night struck a Lake 1 Ml. long which has a Stream, the
same Size as the others falling into its N. End - obliged to go
N. ½ Ml to find where we could pass it. - another small Lake
just above, on this Brook. Saw here the first inhabited
Beaver house we have met with West of Halifax.

    <u>29th</u>. Continued our Course for 6 Ms. first 3 Mls. Small
steep hills, about ½ covered with Beech Oak & white Birch.
Soil tolerably good but too rocky for any thing but Pasture, ½
only Rocks to be seen. Timber small Pine - next 2 Ms. large
Spruce & Hemlock - very rocky last Ml a young Growth chiefly
white Birch - ½ of it has a Mixture of Beech & is not so
stoney but that it might be cultivated - At the End of 1½ Ml
passed Brook, and 1½ farther another Size of F. W. Course
S. At Night passed a third rather less same Course [?
Liverpool] running out of a Lake 1½ Ms. long - Small Lakes on
the other Brooks - obliged to go considerable Distances to
the Right & Left by the Lakes, & by miry impassable places in
the Brooks.

    <u>30th</u>. Continued S. 80 W. for ¾ Ml. & struck a small
Lake, which we followed ¼ Ml. to its N. End, where the
Nictau runs out of it - it is here about the Size of Sackville R.
- 1/.4 Ml. before we struck the Lake passed a Brook running
N. Size of Tremains; from the Shape of the Land I suppose
that this receives the Brook which we passed last Night.
Continued our Course for 2 Ms. & struck the Liverpool Road,
14 Miles from Annapolis River. (N. B. the Liverpool Road is
66 Miles long, beginning to count at the Distance of 2 Miles
from A. [?] R. [?]) at the place where the least Branch of the
Nictau crosses the Road. This branch is about the Size of
Tns. B. & runs as I supposed into the Lake which we stuck
this Morning. Our Provisions were so nearly spent that we
found it necessary to go to the Settlements for Supplies.

31st. Returned & followed the Road will we were 18 Ms. from Annapolis River, where we intent to take the Woods. The Land, from here, for 5 Ms. towards Annapolis, is about ¾ Hard wood, Soil rather gravelly, & too stoney, the remaining ¼ poor, spruce Land, containing some good building timber. The same Description will apply to the Land we passed yesterday before we struck the Road. Next 5 Ms. very good hard wood Land, Soil Loam. then about 3 Miles of Barren rocky Land covered with a small Growth of White Birch, Poplar, Spruce & Pine. After passing this, for 2 Miles (as far as we went) the same loamy hardwood Land. Saw some ledges of hard heavy Slate, but the Stones in general continue the coarse Granit.

Septr 1.   Left the Road and steered S. 65 W for 1 Ml on black Spruce Barrens, when we struck a Lake of which we could see 1½ Ms., but as it is lost among Islands think it longer. from the Height which the Water rises in it We thought it most probably that the main Branch of the Nictau, (which crosses the Road 2 Ms. S. of where we left it,) runs through it we followed it ½ Ml. to its N. End, where a Brook, Size of Tns. runs into it. continued our Course ¾ of a Mile on rocky barren Land, which has some good building Timber on it and struck another Lake above a Ml long, followed it ½ Ml. to its S. end where a Brook size of F. W. runs out of it. - continued our Course 1 Mile farther on black Spruce barrens & come to very good hard wood, on which we proceeded 2 Ms. - ½ Mile from the last Lake passed a third Brook size of F. W. Course S. - 1½ Ms. from this a fourth, Size of Tns. Course S.W. - ½ Ml before we haltd saw 1½ Ms forward & to the Right & Left Land ¾ H.wood Remainder Barrens - a long Lake a Mile S of us laying E. & W.

2d.   Proceeded S. 65 W. for 3 Ms. halted on Account of Rain. Land for 2 Ms. high Hills of hardwood, with rocky vallies between then, which commonly contain some good building Timber. - Last Ml. a Barren covered with a Thicket of scrubbed Spruce. After passing it saw that it was a low

Valley ½ Ml broad between 2 H.wood hills, which we had come quartering across. At the End of ½ Ml. passed a Brook Size of F. W. - At the End of 1½ Ml. a second, & at the End of 2½ a third. These 2 Size of Tns. course of all Southward.

<u>3d</u>.   Continued the same Course 4 Ms. Land a hardwood Hill for 40 Rods; then came down to a low rocky Barren very thick covered with scrubbed black Spruce, which continued till Night, except that about half way we passed a small Hill covered with Pine and white Birch. At Night passed a brook rather less than Sackville R., at the lower End of a lake 1½ Ms long, ¾ Ml. broad, very [? shoal] and full of Rocks: Course of Lake & River S. W. the River within a few Rods falls again into a narrow Lake. Saw a high Hill 3 Miles N. which appears to be covered with Hemlock.

<u>4th</u>.   Proceeded S. 65 E. 4 ½ Ms. - were obliged to travel near as far side[?] to go past Lakes - At the End of 2 Ms. struck a Lake near the S. End which has a Stream running S. E. larger than Sackville at the Lake is 1 Ml, broad, & 2 long, but full of Rocks & Islands; the River falls within [? 190] yards into another Lake 1½ [?] long. - 1 Ml after passing the River struck another Lake 1 Ml. long, near its W. End. Which lies near the S. W. Corner of the Lake we struck first - - 1½ Ml farther struck another 1 Ml long, near its Middle, a Brook runs from its north End into a small Lake which appears to empty into the large Lake we struck first - ½ Ml, farther, struck another near the Middle, & ½ Ml. farther another, each about ¾ Ml. long, with small streams running N.   Land first 3 Miles low Barrens, all Rocks, or mossy Swamps except a ridge of Sand covered with [?] & white Birch about ½ Way between the 2 Rivers, which divides the Barren into 2 Vallies -- Last 2 Ms. chiefly high hardwood Hills between the Lakes, Tops of the Hills good, the tallest Beech on some of them that ever I saw. towards the Bottom rocky & gravelly, which a Mixture of Poplar & white Birch. Could see hardwood hills on the W. side of the Barren, 4 Ms. southward, & 2 Northward.

<u>5th</u>.   Continued S. 65 E. for 9 Ms. Land 1/3 Spruce Swamps, which are not so thick as usual, a few Pieces fit for wild Meadow - Remember small Hills covered in general with a Mixture of white Birch, Poplar, Pine & Spruce with an Undergrowth of Laurel & Whortle. The Pines are seldom more than 1 Foot di.r but may grow large if not destroyed by Fire, as the Remains of a large Growth of Pine are still to be seen not entirely decayed. A few Hills which have a small Mixture of Beech - Soil Gravel & Sand, very stoney. - many places entirely covered with large Rocks. At the End of 2 M.S passed a Lake 1 Ml. across, laying N of our Track - saw no Brook - At the end of 6, 7, & 8 Ms. passed 3 Brooks each about the size of F. W. Course N. saw 2 small Lakes on the Last

<u>6th</u>.   Changed our Course to S. 55 W., and struck a Lake which hindered us more than ½ Day, and obliged us to finally return to near our Camp & go 1 Ml. N or W.: we then followed our Course for 2 Miles, and struck a Lake 1½ Ms. long, lying athwart our Course; we followed it a Mile S. of E. to the Southern End where a Brook size of Tns., runs from it a S. W. course - the large Lake which we struck first has a brook not much larger than F. W. running N. W.   The first Lake which we struck has 2 Beech Hills containing each 100 Acres lying by it - poor for hardwood - ½ way between the 2 Lakes passed a Piece of ½ M broad, & 1 Ml long, covered with young Beech 4 & 6 Inches big - the Remainder a Mixture of Spruce & Hemlock, or small White Birch very rocky. - ½ Way between the Lakes, from a tress saw from N. to S. 60 W., for 8 Miles. Large Hills - ¼ hard Wood, Remainder large Spruce & Hemlock - could not see any of the Vallies in which I should judge from the hard wood, & the size of the Hills that there are many Lakes.

<u>7th</u>.   Proceeded S. 55 W. for 5 Ms. - 1st Mile rocky, covered with large Fir & Spruce - Remainder lower, with small Hills, wholly spruce Barrens - At the End of 1 Mile

passed an old blazed Path, supposed the Shelburne Road; it being much more plainly marked than the Indian Paths commonly are - At the End of 4 Miles passed a Brook larger than Tns. Course W.

8th.   Continued S. 55 W. for 7 Miles, obliged to go 1 Mile S. by a Lake - Land all Black Spruce Thickets, about ½ Swamps. Altho' there is no Earth in most Places, yet the Rocks are generally covered with Turf - no Hills more than 10 Feet high - at the End of 4 Ms. saw S. E. a long Way - all Barrens - N. W. at 6 Ms. passed a brook, size of Tns., Course N. At the end of 6 Ms struck a Lake 1½ Ms. long, Brook size of T. W. Course S, at Night passed another Brook Size of F. W. Course N.

9th.   Proceeded S 55 W. not more than 4 Ms. tho' we travelled the whole Day, it being rainy, & the ground very rough. Land for ½ Ms. covered with large Rocks (20 Feet Dr. & under) which have some Soil among them; a growth of yellow Birch of considerable Size, with a thicket of small Fir below, where we halted, struck a Lake ¾ Ml. long, Course S. W., a Birch Hill of the same King by side of it, the Remainder of our Days walk Black Spruce, ½ Swamps, the upland very rocky & full of Windfalls which had given us but little Trouble for three or 4 Days past. At the End of 2 Ms. passed a Brook, Size of Tns., Course N. W.

10th. Still rainy. Proceeded on our Course 2 Ms. & struck a large cross-shaped Lake which might be 2 Ms. from N. to S. & from E. to W.; followed it ½ Ml. to the N. Point, where a River as large as Little Salmon R. falls into it - Continued our Course for 1 Ml. & struck another Branch of the River, about the same size, Course S. which we rafted over; - 1 Mile farther struck the River again, running N. W., apparently both Branches united. followed the River along its bending Course equal to 1 Mile W. Land ½ Hardwood, being the Hills along the River or Lakes. About ½ the hardwood Land fit for Cultivation; the Remainder too rocky;

the last we passed the Best. The 2d Rr. We passed has about 20 Rods Breadth of very good Land for wild Meadow. In the Bend of the River just above where we halted, about 40 Acres of Marsh & Interval mixed. The softwood Land we passed is chiefly covered with Fir about 6 Inches big, - very stoney - After passing the second River the Stones change to the blue mountain Stone.

11th. Continued our Course for 2 Ms.; 1½ Ms. of it on the River, last ½ Ml. left the River on the left hand, - changed our Course to S. W. and went 10 Ms. farther, on some of the best Ground for travelling we ever met with, which was very fortunate for us as our Provisions were gone. - 2 Miles before we halted passed the middle Stream of Tusket, about the Size of L. Salmon Rr. - Land for the first 5 Miles chiefly soft wood, with but little stone - 1/3 of it barren Gravel thinly covered with Black Spruce, white Reindeer Moss covered the Ground; the Remainder (a little hardwood excepted) a loamy Soil, rather poor and covered with Fir chiefly; this would answer for farming where Meadows could not be connected with it, of which we saw some on the E. Branch. Last 7 Ms. 2/3 high H.wood Hills of middling Quality, pretty dry, and well calculated for Wheat or Rye, the Valleys chiefly Spruce & Fir, not very stoney, contained some good building Timber, & a few large Spars 2½ Feet Dr., but which will not in general run more than 60 Feet - 1 Ml. before we halted touched a Lake 1 Ml. long, on our Right which has a Brook a Size of Tns running from it into the middle Branch.

12th. Continued S. W. for 1 Ml. in thick Spruce Land. when observing that the same Kind of Land continud for a considerable Distance, changed our Course to S. hoping from the goodness of the Land, that we should soon find Settlers on the Tusket; proceeded 9 Miles to Mr. Rayners at Tusket Falls, last 3 Ms. along the Side of a lake of the Middle Branch which is 6 Ms. long and which ends here - it is 6 Ms. from here to the Salt water, almost all the way Lake - a bad Fall at the Mouth - the East Branch falls into the Lake 1½ Ms. below Mr. Rds. And the little W. Branch falls into the bay of Salt Water below the place where the large River falls into it. Land till within 1½ Ms. of Mr. Rds. the same as the latter Part of yesterdays walk; it then grows worse & more rocky.

13th. Employed in procuring Provisions. Mr. Raynerd who took us down to the Settlement in his Boat, assisted us to procure what we needed among the Inhabitants. The Land is very rocky and poor near the Salt Water. There is a French Village below here where the People live entirely upon Eels & Potatoes, One of the most able of them assured me that most of the French Families did not use 4 Pounds of Flour in a year. they keep Sheep enough to make their own Clothing, & the Meat & Butter which they sell supplies them with the little money they need, - They tell me that they often catch 30 Barrels of Eels in a Night in the Brook they live upon - Mr. Rd. showed us a narrow Passage in the Lake below his house where a Party of the French who had retired to the Place where he lives, laid an Ambush for a Party of Soldiers who were sent to remove them. They lay on three Points each of which is within short Gunshot of the Place marked [?] o, & in that very Spot the Bargemen stopped & lay upon their Oars for the Soldiers to dine, which gave the French an Opportunity to take a more exact Aim, so that they killed the greatest Part of them.

14th. Set out Late and went 2 Ms. to Salmon Rr., the W. Branch of the Tuskets. Followed it up for 1 Ml., it has commonly 30 Roads Breadth of Swamp which could make wild Meadow. This as well as the other Branches is chiefly still Water or Lakes.

15th. Steered N. Easterly to the Middle Branch, followed it till about 9 Ms. above Mr. Rds there is a hardwood Ridge almost always by the side of the River, but in some places it is separated from it by ½ Ml of Spruce Land - there is hard wood likewise generally by side of Most of the small

Lakes which lie on the Small Streams that fall into the River, but the greatest Part of the Land within 2 Ms. of the middle Branch is soft Wood, part of which is Swamp that would make wild Meadow we passed this Day about 40 Acres in one Piece upon a Small Brook which would make good wild Meadow. ½ Ml. before we halted passed a Brook size of Tns. running into the River.

16. Steered N. for 6 Ms.; then turned N. 60 E. for 2 Ms. but did not reach the River, Land except 1 Ml. hwood all Spruce & Fir, not very stony, very flat, so that we could not see any Distance. Very bad Travelling, as there is almost every where a Thicket of small Fir, which conceals a Multitude of Windfall so that we had no Chance to Pick our Way among them.

17th. Came to the River within ¼ Ml.; saw from a Tree on a Hill that there was a H.Wood Hill on the E. side of the River a great way below us. on the W. side of the Hwood is 1½ Ms. back - Followed the river, which is very crooked, for Distance which we judged to be equal to 2 Ms. N. - then 3 Miles farther N. E. chiefly upon a large Lake - hard wood most of the Way for this 3 Ms. close to the River on both Sides, - saw some trees on this large Lake marked with a cross which appeared to have been done very long ago. - soon after passing the Lake the River turned S. of E. and we travelled E. for 2 Ms. but did not reach the River - Land first Ml H.wood, last Spruce. - where we halted we could see H.wood on almost every Side from 1 to 2 Ms. Distance - saw this Day about 100 Acres of Land on the River which would make wild Meadow, but no dry Interval –

18th. Came to the River within ¼ Ml., followed it up, general course N.E., for 8 Ms. - about half the way by its side, leaving it at Times when very crooked. Left it on the Right 1½ Ms. before we halted. at which Place it was about the Size of Tns. - ½ Ml. farther passed a Branch of it not quite half so large, coming from the N.W. - Land for 6½ Ms.

¾ Spruce, containing considerable good Timber. - few Spars above 16 Inches - Remaining ¼ Hardwood, rather poor Soil with a Mixture of Spruce - Hills but little elevated, which prevented us from seeing any considerable Distance; what we could see like what we were upon - saw 100 Acres of Meadow on the river - (no Interval.) - a few Acres clear of Bushes (we had been informed that a Number of the French had formerly retired to some place near here where they could make Hay for their Cattle, and that they continued here for 18 Months) - next Mile, very good H.wood. - last ½ Ml. Spruce Barrens.

19th. Proceeded N. for 8 Ms. - first 6 Ms. 2/3 very good Hardwood – remaining 1/3, thick Swamps edged with good Spruce Timber, Swamps mostly poor, - hardwood hills considerably elevated above them - last 2 Ms. half Spruce, the hardwood Hills not so high, nor so good as the other - Soil of all the hard wood dry, and rather gravelly, very little stone. At the End of 3 Ms. struck a Lake 1½ Ms. long, which has a Brook size of F. W. falling into its E End.   (N.B. from this Lake we found a Bear path going W. of N. which we followed as we had been turned near a Ml. E by the Lake & miry Brook which falls into it: after following it for 1½ Ms. Came to an open Barren of Peat, containing perhaps 40 Acres, full of Paths made by Moose, Bears and Caribou; the 2 latter had been here last Night. There are a great Number of deep holes containing Water which these Animals frequent, which cause the Paths: in several of them I could only perceive the common disagreeable Taste of Swamp Water, but one had a strong Bilge water Taste, of which I supposed there must be some Tincture in the other, tho' I did not perceive it. I saw a little yellow Ochre in one of them. We saw the Bones of 2 Moose by 2 of them (surprised probably by Bears whilst they were drinking). All the small Rivulets we pass run to the W.

20th. Observed from a Tree that the Land for 8 Ms. W. appeared to be all Spruce - N. we could see 6 Ms. - no hardwood, but what was mixed with Spruce. - E. could see hard wood within a Mile. Observed a very distant, round Hill N. 10 W. Proceeded N. E. for 4 Ms. & struck S. Rr. At a great Fall. Land Spruce & Hemlock with a Mixture of Hwood. a good hard wood Hill half the Way on our Right. Within ½ Mile of the River the Land becomes very stoney which it had not been before. The Fall in the River is equal to 25 Feet perpenr.   it falls at an Angle of about 60 degrees The River is here 6 or 7 Rods broad. Followed Rr. For 4 Ms. to the Head of The Ride, Course a little S. of W. very rough rocky Banks, often above 100 Feet high, The River is rapid and full of Rocks and has a bad Fall just above the Tide; it is larger than Preston Big S. R. saw this Day a Number of Spruce Spars 2 Feet big & 60 in Length - From Mr. Rayners to Sissabou Falls we met with no Impediment to a Road except the universal ones of Swamps & Lakes - neither a bad Hill nor any considerable Distance of very rocky Land.

    <u>21st</u>. Came down the River for 3 Ms. to Col Moodys as he was absent from Home, followed the Road 6 Miles Eastward to Mr. Northups where we supplied ourselves with Provisions.

    <u>22d</u>.   Set out from Mr. Ns. & travelled S. E. for 8 Ms. - Land for 6 Ms. generally covered with a Mixture of Spruce, Hemlock, Beech, Birch, & Maple of both kinds. Soil gravelly, not very stoney, about the same Quality as the Land which is cultivated at Sissabou, but more level. Next Mile very rocky, with the coarse Granite, covered only with large Spruce - last Mile a low Barren covered with scrubbed Spruce & small Bushes. - Till this Evening the Stones had always been the blue mountain Stone & Slate with a small Mixture of Granite, ever since we left the Falls of Tusket, but we observed that the other side of St Marys Bay had a Bank of red Stone, which we were informed was good Freestone. At the End of 5 Ms. passed a Brook, Size of Tns., Course S. W.

23d.   Proceeded S. E. 2 Ms. changed our Course to N. 70 E. and went 2 Ms. farther - at the End of ½ Ml. passed a Stream Size of Sackville River, - at the End of 2 Ms. touched another which we supposed to be the main Branch of S. R. tho' we could not ascertain its size, as it was dead Water, the Ground being marshy. Land almost all Barrens - last 2 Ms. covered with large Rocks, the Swamps excepted. - Observed from Trees that there were some Hills of hardwood on the S. side of the last River. Moose Tracks uncommonly frequent this Day.

24th. Proceeded upon different Courses equal to 6 Ms, N. 70 E. - At the end of 1½ Miles passed the Streams we touched yesterday at a place where 2 Brooks which make it unite; each about the size of F. W., and ½ Ml. above a Lake 1 Ml. long - Land on our Course Barrens, covered with large Rocks, except the Swamps some small hardwood hills near the Lake, Mixed Beech & Spruce Hills commonly about 1½ Ms. N. of our Course - At the End of 4 Ms. observed that the Land from E. to S. was covered with Spruce and Pine from 5 to 8 Ms. - at those Distances Hills which have some spots mixed with Hardwood

25th. Continued N. 70 E. for 3 Ms., changed our Course to N. E. for 3 Ms. farther - At the End of ½ Mile passed a Brook, Size of Tns., Course Northward - at the End of 3 Ms. a second same size & course, at Night a third rather larger, observed the Course of the Valley in which it runs to be between W. & N. W. for 4 Ms. below where we passed it - By climbing a Number of Trees saw the Land within 2 Ms. on each Side - The Brooks run in broad barren rockey Vallies, with narrow Hills (interrupted in some places) running parralel to them - the highest Points of these Hills Breech Land, rather poor - more than 4/5 of the Land, barren, covered with large Granite Rocks - the last Mile we came over one of the roughest Pieces of rocky Ground we ever passed - The Timber after passing the first Brook, a first Growth after a Fire, consisting of white Birch, Small Spruce

& Pine chiefly - The Hill on the N. side of the last Brook is the highest, and is covered apparently wholly with white Birch.

26th. Continue N. E. for 1 Ml. then turned N. as our Provisions would only last this Day. followed that Course for 5 Miles & struck a Path, which we followed, a N. W. course for 1½ Ms. - Land for 3 Miles chiefly covered with white Birch - ½ of it too rocky, and ¾ of it too poor for Cultivation - ¼, better with a mixture of young Beech & yellow Birch - next Mile high Beech Hills. then for 1½ Ms. extremely rough Hills covered with Rocks from 10 to 20 Feet Dr. with a Growth of Spruce & white Birch. Remainder, white Birch Land of a better Quality than we passed in the Morning, having commonly a Mixture of Beech but pretty stoney - At the End of 4 Ms. on our last course passed a Brook Size of F. W. which I saw followed a nearly N. W. Course for 4 Ms. passed afterwards 2 small Streams which appeared to run to this - all the latter part of our Days Walk high Hills.

27. Followed the Path for 1 Mile to the Settlement of Clements, took the Road from there, for 4 Miles when we struck the main Road at the Mouth of the Moose River; the Stream which we struck yesterday. followed the Road for 8 Miles to Annapolis - The best Land begins within 3 Miles of the Shore and continues some way towards it - equal to good Hardwood Land - We have been informed that on Moose River within 3 Miles of the Shore there is a large Bed of Iron Ore; Its late Proprietor sent a few Barrells of it to Boston to be Assayed, & was informed that it was good.

28th. Employed in Writing and other necessary Business.

29th. Employed in Writing & providing Necessaries most of the day, set out late & went 2 Miles up the Brook which falls in here. Course a little E. of S.

<u>30th</u>. Left the Brook & steered S. E. for 6 Miles, then N. 80 E. for 1 Mile. Land for the first 2 Ms. very rocky & poor, originally Pine Land, mostly. Next 4½ Ms. covered chiefly with white Birch, A few Ridges with a Mixture of Beech, & a few small Swamps; making together ¼ of the whole which are tolerable Land, the Remainder very rocky, with a Soil of coarse, white Gravel. next 1½ Ms. Beech Land of a middle Quality mixed in some Places with white Birch. Soil Gravel. At the Place where we turned saw that the Land between S. 30 E., & S. 30 W. was chiefly Hardwood or white Birch for 2 & 3 Ms.; beyond those Distances some Softwood Hills (apparently Pine) appeared, till the last Ml. before we turned the Land was generally rising very slowly. Directly upon turning struck the N. End of a Lake near a Mile long which had a small Brook running S. W. from it. 2 Ms. back had passed a small Rivulet running S. - after leaving the Lake, Land, and black spruce Barrens.

<u>Octob. 1st</u>.   Proceeded N. 80 E. for 9 Miles - about a Middle of this Distance passed 1½ Ms. of tolerable Beech Land, on a high Ridge between 2 deep Valleys which have each a small Rivulet in them running N. - The Remainder of the Land covered with Black Spruce chiefly, 6 & 8 Inches big, in some places a Mixture of Fir, Birch & Poplar, most of it very rocky, the last Mile chiefly a solid Rock without any soil except Turf - at the End of 6 Miles passed a Brook near the Size of F. W. & at Night touched a small Lake with a very small Brook - Course of both N.- At the End of 1 Ml. observed Spruce Land to reach 1½ Ms. N., then white Birch. - S. it reaches 1 Mile, then rough Hills, part of which have Hardwood on their Tops. At the End of 6 Ms. observed the Spruce Land to reach 3 Ms. S., then Hills of which some are a Mixture of hard & soft Wood, others all soft Wood.

<u>2d.</u>   Continued N. 80 E. for 10 Miles. At the End of 1 Ml. came to a hardwood Ridge ½ Ml. broad. At the End of 4 Ms. came to a lake 1 Ml. long with a small brook, Course N. - 2 Hills about 1½ Ms. apart bound the barren Valley which

this runs in; they have each about ¼ Miles breadth of hard wood of the Top as far as I could see (about 3 Ms. N. & 2 S.) almost all the Remainder of our Days Walk black Spruce, about 6 Inches big. In some places a solid Rock only covered with Turf, in others loose Rocks, in others a Mixture of Rocks & coarse Gravel. At the End of 5 Ms. observed that the Land for 4 Ms. southward had some H.Wood Hills, but was more than ¾ Spruce - At the End of 7 Ms. passed a Brook size of F. W. Course S. - For the last 3 Ms. observed Hardwood Northward at the Distance of 2 Miles.

<u>3d.</u>   Continued our Course for 2 Ms. to the Ll. Road 13 Ms. from As. Rr. - Stoney birch Land till within ½ Ml. of the Road, when it changes to Beech - ½ Ml. before we struck the Road, crossed the little Branch of the Nictau, Course S., observed that it continued N. for 1½ Ms. to a Lake, the Hardwood Ridge of the Brook the same which the Road runs upon. followed the Road down to the Settlement. (Caribou Tracks more frequent these 3 Days past than we have observed in any other Place.)

I am informed by Mr. Parker that to steer West from Liverpool Road, (setting out about 2 Ms. N. of where the little Branch of the Nictau crosses it) for 7 Miles & then turn N. to the As. River, will enclose a Piece of Land which is almost all good. that beyond the little Branch for 6 Miles the good Land is not broad enough for more than 1 Tier of Lots. That from the little Branch down to the Settlements, the Land between the Road and the Nictau (about 2 Miles breadth on an Average) is chiefly good; that the Land is chiefly good for 3 or 4 Ms. back & as far as he has travelled East (4 Miles) of the Township Line the Land is chiefly good, that farther up the River (after going 2 or three Miles on bad Land) is a Ridge about 3 Ms. long & ½ Mile broad, laying parrallel to the River. Mr. Parker says that he is well acquainted with the Land above described, having often traversed it in Hunting; the Accounts he gives of the Waters & Brooks back of this agree perfectly with what I have observed. & he is a Man to whom I should give the most entire Credit, judging from his Countenance & Conversation.

[As = Annapolis; Tns = Tremain's; F.W. = Fresh Water]

Sawmill Creek about 3 Miles from As.		Size of Tns.
Round Hill	7 Ms.	F.W.
Bloody Creek*	15 Ms.	Tns.
Button Creek	18	F. W.
	19	F. W.
Paradise	21	Tns.
Lunns Mills	23	F. W.
	23¼	F. W.
	24	F. W.
Lovats Brook	25	F. W.
Little Nictau	28	Tns.
Big Nictau	30	

*or Eell Weir, named from the Circumstance of a Number of People being killed here by the Indians

Mr. Wheelock informed us that the largest Tract of good Land he knows of, is on the E. Side of La Haive; and about half way to Lunenburg; it is of an uncommon good Quality and continues for a considerable Length, but he did not examine its Breadth, that the Brook which we passed directly before we struck the Nictau (on our 3d Course) & a very small one & something nearer to As. R. than to the southern sea coast, that the Largest Lake of La Haive is about half way to Lunenburg & that there are 2 or 3 Lakes between that and the Falls of La Haive. His Plan of these Lakes & others belonging to the Two Rivers is drawn by an Indian, and he has verified the greatest Part of it by his own Observations.

We are informed by many Persons that there is Iron Ore in many Places in the S. Mountain, near here. Iron Works have been erected here, & the Iron which was forged is said to have been of good Quality, but the Business failed on Account of the Proprietor's not having a Capital sufficient to carry it on. The Iron Works are at present the Property of Brook Watson. The Vein of Ore which they worked runs in a straight Line, in a Rock of Slate, it is between 2 & 3 Feet broad its Length & Breadth are unknown.

There is an Indian here who has been at Work this Season and raised a small Crop of Corn, Wheat & Potatoes, and who is very desirous of continuing to work at farming, but his Countrymen have taken as much Pains to divert him from the miserable Kind of Life which they fancy he must lead, as white Men could have done to prevent one of their Friends from living with the Indians; His Squaw was always uneasy and finally ran away from him into the Woods. he followed her & after being gone for Five or Six Weeks returned with her lately. He still persists in his Resolution to be a Farmer, but most probably his Countrymen will finally persuade him to quit his new Occupation, as he will be accounted an Indian by white Men, and if he follows farming, will be looked upon as a white Man by Indians.

4th.   Employed in providing for the Woods.

5th.   Followed the Road which is on the E. Side of the Nictau   S. Course till near 8 Ms. from As. R. - turned N. 80 E & proceeded 3 Ms. - Hardwood Land as far as we followed the Road, after leaving it, first & third Mile rocky barren Land, 2d. Ml. Hardwood, at the end of the 2d Ml. observed that the Land was almost all Soft Wood near to a S. E. Course for 5 Ms. - At the Place where we left the Road passed a Brook, Size of F. W. course N. E.

6th.   Proceeded N. 80 E. for 6 Ms. First 3 Ms. barren gravelly Land chiefly covered with Rocks, Timber Pine & Spruce, containing some good Timber for Building - the Pines not bigger than 16 Inches -Last 3 Ms. ¼ Hardwood, rather Stoney, Soil gravelly Remainder a Mixture of Beech, Spruce & Hemlock; Soil inferior to that of the Hardwood - At the End of 2 Miles passed a Brook Size of F. W. Course N. E., At Night struck a Lake 2 Ms. long with a Brook size of F. W. Course N. At the End of 3 Ms. observed that we have come quartering across a barren Valley in which the Brook runs. It is here 2 Ms. Broad, down Stream it grows narrower, its Course N. E., up Stream it increases in Breadth Course S. barren Land on that Course for 5 Ms. a Hardwood Hill every where on its N. W. side. ½ Ml. before we halted observed that for 4 Ms. N. E., 3 S. E., & 2 E. & N. the Land is chiefly covered with a Mixture of Hard & soft Wood. a few small Pieces of both unmixed.

7th.   Obliged to go 1 M. N. by the lake, then proceeded, Course S. 80 E. for 4 Ms. & struck a Lake 2 Ms. long, followed it for 1 Ml. to its N. E. End a Brook Size of F. W. runs N. from it, it runs out about ½ Mile from the N. E. End.

The 2 Lakes lie each of them in a flat Valley about 1 M. broad, no Soil but loose Rocks. - covered with Pine, black Spruce & white Birch. About half way between the Lakes a Valley 1½ Miles broad, all Rocks, Timber, small yellow Pine & black Spruce. The Remainder consists of 2 Ridges covered with large Spruce & Hemlock with a mixture of hardwood, extremely rocky. On the very Tops of the Hills a small Breadth chiefly Beech, Soil good, but 1/3 covered with Rocks. ½ Mile before we struck the last Lake observed that the Land was all Soft wood for 5 Ms. N. E. & that the Tops of the 2 Hills which the Lake lies between are mixed with H.wood all its Length - In the middle Valley abovementioned passed 2 Brooks Size of F. W., Course N. The large Ridges are not regular Hills but covered every where with small steep Hills, made by Heaps and loose Rocks or Swells of the Solid Rock. Windfalls from the great Storm very troublesome these 2 Days past - Stones on the Hills wholly the coarse Granite. in the Valleys 1/3 the blue mountain Stone, some of which contains a great deal of sulphurous Iron ore.

8th.   Followed the Lake till we had recovered our Course 1 Ml. forward of where we struck the Lake.

Proceeded 4 Ms. & struck another Lake of which we saw about 2 Ms. in Length. Followed it 1 Ml. to the N. End, recovered our Course & proceeded till we had advanced 3 Miles from where we struck the Lake. Land for 2 Miles barren gravelly Soil covered with small black Spruce & white Birch, or Spruce Swamp, then same upon a high hardwood Hill which continued for 2 Ms. farther. Remainder the same as the first 2 Ms., last Ml. excepted, which is covered with large white Birch & Poplar. & might ½ of it be cultivated the other ½ too rocky. The Lake we struck has another beginning within 100 yards N. of it which is 3 or 4 Ms. long. There is no Fall between them but as the Water is now low, there is not more than enough for an Indian Canoe. The general Course of the Lakes I judge to be N. 20 E. the hardwood Hill which we passed continue nearly the Length of both. - Another as long, parrallel to it 4 or 5 Ms. E. - could not at that distance tell whether it is Beech or white Birch.   1 Ml. before we halted passed a Brook larger than F. W. Course N. E.

9th.   Continued S. 80 E. for 7 Ms.; obliged to go 1 M. S. by Lakes - At the End of 2 Ms. passed a Brook Size of Tns., Course N., a Chain of small Lakes on it for 4 Ms. down. at that distance the deep Valley in which is runs is stopped by a high H.Wood Hill which there appears to lie E. & W. but 2 Ms from there its E. End bends to the S. - 1½ Ms. farther struck a triangular Lake 1½ Ms long, on much higher Land than the Brook we came from.   the Stream comes in at its E. point and runs out at the N. - after going ½ Ml. S. to pass it, proceed 2 Ms. & struck another 2 Ms. long & 1½ broad, went S. for ½ Ml. to pass this, and proceeded 1½ Ms. & struck the Brook a little above where it falls into the Lake it is about the size of Tns. - Land, for the first 3 Miles very rocky & poor, covered chiefly with small white Birch & black Spruce - Remainder almost all fit for Cultivation, about ½ Hardwood, the other ½ a Mixture of Fir, Maple, & white & yellow Birch - a hardwood Hill on the N. E. side of the Lakes likewise.

<u>10th</u>. Proceeded N. 80 E. for 9 Ms. - At the End of 5 Miles struck an irregular Lake, the Branches of which occupy a Space of 2 Ms. E. & W., & 1½ Ms. N. & S. - a Brook Size of Tns. runs Course N. E. Land; very high Hills on all Sides, - First Ml. a barren rocky Valley, except that it contains considerable of good Alder Swamp, then for ½ Ml. a high Beech Hill, very good - ½ Ml. of Hardwood near the Lake, - last Ml. black Spruce chiefly Swamp. Remainder white Birch, mixed often with Spruce or Fir. About 1/8 of this Land Alder Swamp in pieces of 3 or 4 Acres commonly, - ½ the Remainder too rocky for Cultivation. The other half has a sandy Soil, and would do for Farms, tho' not equal to the hardwood. Observed that the Hardwood reached 2 Ms. up the Brook we l eft this Morning, on the E. Side. - on the W. Side a Hill for the same Distance mixed Fir & Birch, a little Beech on the Summit the Hills continued some Ms. farther, but could not distinguish the Timber as the Weather was hazy - There are near 1000 Acres of Beech on the S. W. Sides of the Lake. - Observed that the Land for several Miles on each Side of our Course had some scattered Beech Hills but far the greatest Part is a Mixture of White Birch & soft Wood.

<u>11th</u>. Proceeded N. 80 E. for 6 Ms., then E. for 3 Ms and struck the S. Branch of Pisaquid River about 6 Ms. from Windsor - Land for 2 Ms. white Birch & Fir about ½ fit for Cultivation, then passed a Brook larger than Tns., Course N. E. after passing this ascended a very high, rocky Hill on which we continued till we came to the Valley in which the S. Branch runs - Land all bad, very little soil on the Granite Rock which forms the Mountain, - Timber small white Birch & black Spruce.

<u>12th</u>. Came to Windsor, were informed by Mr. Schwartz that Mr. John Walker at Falmouth could direct us to the good Land on the Head of Pisaquid River went to Falmouth - were informed by Mr. W. that the 2 Brooks which we passed the 10th & 11th form the N. Branch of Pr Rr,. & unite about 4 Ms. above the Tide - gave us what Directions

he could to find the Land, which he thought to be very good, & to contain a Quantity equal to 4 Ms. Square.

13th. After supplying ourselves with Provisions left Windsor and went 8 Miles. (till we were above 2 Ms. above the Tide on the S. Branch)

14th   Followed the Rr. Till we judged we had proceeded 6 Ms. Course between S. & S. W. - for 3 Ms above the Tide the River runs between 2 Mountains & has generally a little poor Interval. at that distance there is a Fall of about 40 Feet in the Distance of 6 Rods. The Water falls in a winding Manner over a Ledge of the blue Mountain Stone altho' the Hills on each Side are Granite. - above this Fall the Hill are more moderate - There is high Beech hill on the E. Side of the Rr, which begins ½ Ml. below our camp and reaches ¾ Mls. above it, about ½ Ml. broad - 1 Ml. S. E. of this lies another (across a barren valley) 1 Ml. long & ¼ Ml. broad as I judged from a Distance. On the W. side of the River for 1 Ml. above our Camp & ¾ Ml back from the Rr. the Land is ½ Beech. Remainder Spruce & white Birch. - a little below this went a Mile W. from the River, Land chiefly Rocky Barrens. - The Hardwood on the E. Side is pretty stoney & very dry, but appears to be Land of good Strength by the Size & Height of the Trees. - 1½ Ms. below us lies a Lake ¾ Ml. long - The sides of the Hills next the River for 30 or 40 Rods breadth are very rocky & covered with good Spruce Timber. between here & the Falls there is generally about the same Breadth covered with Fir & white Birch with but little Stone. farther back very rocky.

15th. Lay still most of the Day on Account of rain - near Night followed the Brook up ¼ Ml., then went a little N. or W. for 1 Ml. most of the way by side of a Branch which contains ½ the Brook & is as large as Tns. At the distance of 1 Ml. from the other it turns N. W. & divides into 3 parts. Observed from a very tall Tree that the Land N. W. of the River is mixed with Hardwood for 2 Ms. N. W. - 1/3 clear

Hardwood, 1/3 Hemlock & Spruce 18 Inches big & under, very tall - 1/3 Spruce Swamps & rocky Valleys, - the Beech continues farther N. W. but with a much greater Proportion of Spruce. - could not see above 1 Ml. S. W. Observed the general Course of the River below to be near N. E. altho' I could not come near Exactness as the Rocking of the Tree prevented the Compass from Settling. The Land covered with large Spruce is not so stoney but that it may be cultivated.

16th. Proceeded S. 20 W. for 1 Ml, then S. W. for ¾ Ml., then S. 60 E. for 4 Ms. and struck the Chester Road; - Marked 2 Spruces on the E. Side of the Road with a W and followed the Road 1 Ml. towards Windsor; finding no Mile marks left it and went 2 Ms. S. 80 E. Land for the first 1¼ Ms. Alternately hard & soft Wood, next Mile Rocky Barrens, then Hardwood for 1 Mile, from there to the Road rocky Land covered with large Spruce, after leaving the Road ½ the same Spruce, the other granite Barrens, on the Top of a very high Hill - Could not see any Hardwood farther S. W. than the Place where we turned Eastward, tho' we could not see a great Distance, the day being rainy, - within the first 2 Ms. passed 7 or 8 small Brooks which contain the Remainder of this Branch of the Brook, - saw about 50 Acres of Alder Swamp on them. - ½ Mile before we struck the Road passed the other Branch, which separates from that we had been following at the Lake. mentioned the 14th - ½ the Hardwood which we passed this Day is a small Growth of yellow Birch & Beech, the Ground covered with Ground-Hemlock. the other half a large growth of Beech.

17th. Mr. Carter being sick lay still part of the Day. - Proceeded S. 80 E. for 5 Ms. - At the End of 1 & 3 Ms. passed 2 Brooks, Size of F. W. Course S. E. a little rocky Hardwood Land near each of them . Remainder of the Land for 4 Ms. rocky Barrens - At the End of 4 Ms passed a Lake of St. Croix River, apparently near its lower End, could see up it, course S. 30 W. for 4 Ms. - some small pieces of beech, but almost

all the Land on the Hills which bound it, white Birch &
Spruce. - after passing the Lake, large Spruce - all Land near
our Course mountainous Hills.

18th. Continued S. 80 E. for 7 Ms. - At the End of 1
Mile passed a Brook Size of Tns. at the End of 3, 5, & 6 Ms.
passed three Brooks, Size of F. W.; Course of all, Southward.
saw Lakes upon all of them. Land all Mountainous; first 4
Miles large Spruce, very little Soil on the Rock. last 3 Ms.
1/3 Hardwood, (Soil very good, but very stoney,) laying near
the Tops & on the East Sides of the Hills, the W. Sides &
Valleys almost wholly Rock - At Night struck a narrow
crooked Lake of which we could not see either End. -
Abundance of Timber blown down, ever since we left the
Head of Pisaquid River –

19th. Followed the Lake, 1¼ Ms. to the Head, Course
a little E. of N., within ½ Ml. of the Head of Brook coming
from the N. W. falls into it. at the Head another coming from
the N. E., each about the Size of Tns. - Proceeded E. for 5
Ms. & Struck the Road 24 Ms. from Halifax; followed it Home
- Land to the Road very rocky, covered chiefly with large
Spruce & Hemlock - saw several small Lakes with little
Rivulets running Southward. - The Stones in the hardwood
Land on the Head of the Pisaquid River are the blue
mountain Stone from there always the coarse Granit till
within one Mile of the Windsor road when they change to
Slate & the blue mountain Stone. - The Weather for some
days has been rainy & so hazy that I could not see any
considerable Distance.

GENERAL OBSERVATIONS on the WESTERN TOUR

In the whole course of our Western Tour, we have constantly found the best land to be upon hills which lie by the sides of and run parallel to, the lakes and rivers, so that the course which was traced for us, and which obliged us to cross all the streams, was undoubtedly the best to ascertain the real proportion of good and bad land, though more difficult for us to follow, than a contrary direction would have been (see August 29th). To have passed a number of small lakes, which I have not noticed, as they had no streams of any consequence from them.

We have seldom passed a night in the woods but we have perceived, by cry of the loons, that there were lakes near us, which we did not see; and I believe, there are but few places in the Western part of the province which have not a lake within a mile of them, except very near the sea coast--The mountaineous land, which reaches from Margaret's Bay to Windsor and which lies back of Falmouth and Horton and continues from thence nearly to Sissabou, forming what is called the South mountain appears to be a continuity of solid hills of granite, in some places without any earth upon it, but most commonly with some soil. Even the rich loamy land upon the Nictaw has many naked swells of rock in it. There is no part of this land extremely poor, where there is a sufficient depth of soil nor cultivation. Near Shelburne, the soil is very barren, even when sufficiently deep, among rocks of nearly the same kind (granite) mixed with the blue stone; but both the rocks and the soil, continue a large quantity of Isinglass, which is not the case with the land above mentioned.

The large tract of level land between Liverpool and Jordan Rivers contains some valuable meadows, but no upland, but what it extremely barren. A great proportion of this land is mostly swamps, which were once shallow lakes, and have been filled up with mud. I think from the success of small experiments, Colonel Bayard (Annapolis River) had a swamp covered with hackmatack and hardhack (Larsh spiros frutex) which produced a little wild grass, a muddy soil 2 feet deep on a hard bottom. An English soldier employed by the Colonel asserted that he could make good land of this swamp, and obtained permission of the Colonel to try. He drained the swamp and burnt the moss and bushes. It has this year been sowed with different kinds of grain and produced a most luxuriant crop. Colonel Bayard has since refused 60 bushels of clean wheat offered to him for an acre and three quarters of that grain as it stood on the ground. It is supposed it will yield 40 bushels to the acre. T.L.

It is very certain that all kinds of swamps and mossy boggs, may be rendered very productive, [? if] pains suitable to their qualities are taken: the proper method is to run a trench round them, in order to cut off the water from the high lands, then having discovered where the vent is, make a wide drain from thence through the middle, at the vent the surrounding and middle drains should unite, but not so at the head by several feet. Lateral and diagonal, very small should unite with the wide middle drain in all directions. The surrounding drain should be deeper than the middle drain at the vent, that the water of the former may not run into the latter. The drains should all be wider at top than bottom. [?} should vent in which I have tried on this kind of swamps, that they may be made to produce very large crops, by draining and a little manure, but that they will never continue fruitful for a great length of time without manure, as is the case with the swamps, made by the mud washed from a rich soil.

I should think that the swamps which lie back of Shelburne, are the most valuable land near that place. Those which have but a small depth of mud are the best as they can be drained at the least expense. Seaweed and seamud have a greater effect on this kind of land than any other manure I have seen tried.

I do not think there is any quantity of good upland in the Liverpool River.

But I have reason to think that Port Medway River has some good land, by the side of it, from the place where it crosses the Liverpool road to its head.

Eastward of this river, there are no such large tracts of barrens, as there are westward, but the good land, usually has the disadvantage of laying in small tracts, which are not large enough for a considerable number of settlers adjoining each other.

The best situations for roads as well as land will commonly be found by following the courses of the streams. The large tract of spruce land, which lies above the Head of Margaret's Bay, is so mountainous and rocky that it must be extremely difficult to make any carriage road through it, but I do not think there would be much difficulty in making winter roads as there are a great number of lakes on the streams which run through it. There is on this land a very great quantity of excellent timber and a considerable number of spars, suitable for mast timber, although there are not many of a large size. We observed near the large lake on the head of Liverpool River, plants which grow in the southern States, and we have not in any other part of this province. The wild fruit was ripe about 3 weeks sooner than near Annapolis River. There is an Indian at Nictaw who has been at work this season, and raised a small crop of corn, wheat and potatoes and who is very desirous of continuing his new occupation: but his countrymen have taken as much pains to divert him from the miserable kind of life which they fancy he must lead as white men could have done to prevent one of their friends living with the Indians. His squaw who was always uneasy, finally ran away from him into the woods, he followed her and after being gone five or six weeks, he has lately returned with her. He still persists in his resolution to be a farmer, but most probably his countrymen will finally persuade him to quit his new occupation, as he will be accounted an Indian by white men and if he follows farming, will be looked upon as a white man by Indians.

We have found it impossible to converse with the few Indians we have met with owing to their suspicious temper which renders them afraid of strangers. We have met with a very few instances of Indians who have undertaken to cultivate the ground, and to work with some industry, but where they do it gives great uneasiness to their relations and countrymen, who use every means to disengage them from their new occupation and seem to have as strong a prejudice against our way of living as we can have against theirs. There are numbers of Indians in some places employed in the fisheries which seems to please them better than farming (see August 11, Sept. 10).

In every part of the province where we have been, we generally found those who followed fishing complaining of poverty and a herd country: whilst those who depend entirely on farming generally hold an opposite language and appear very well satisfied with their situations, and sensible that they are in a thriving condition--it is probable that good land enough may be found on the Liverpool Road (Augt. 10th, 11th, 12th)to settle 100 families by going 8 miles N. and 4 miles S. of Mr. Burken (Aug. 11th) including the land within 2 miles of the road on each side: at 100 acres each.

Between the stations of August 12th and 15th a distance of 20 miles, we passed 7 miles of good land, different pieces-- this supposing it to hold the same proportion for 3 miles on each side of course, would be sufficient for 268 farms of 100 acres each. A considerable proportion of this land is moist and very good for grass. It is very easy to make a good road upon our track from the Liverpool road to the bank of the La Have River, but the river runs in a very deep valley, not easily passed in those places where we struck it. The stone on this land is almost entirely slate, which appears to be of a good kind for splitting as the [? Lamina] are regular: and it shows no ironrust like the state near Halifax.

I have seen Mr. Wheelock's plan of La Have River, and as far as a I remember, the largest body of good land which he has seen lies about 8 or 10 miles N. of where we passed it. On the 27th of August when we passed the streams which form part of the Eastern branch of La Have River we saw considerable quantities of hardwood land on the hills which lay by the sides of the brooks: and I think it most probable that it continues down to the where we passed the river on the 15 Augt.

The Indians assert that it is good land on Port Midway River, continued for 20 miles above where it crossed the Liverpool road. This is rendered probable by what we observed on the 4th of September where we passed this river, there being a hardwood hill on the west side of it as far as we could see.

On the Tuskets and along our track from the 9th to the 19 of September, there probably is good land enough for 300 farms besides a considerable quantity of softwood land, which may finally be cultivated as it is not very stony, but which would not answer for new settlers.

There is abundance of good timber for building almost everywhere upon this land. There are many groves of fir near the Tuskets, which have uncommon quantity of balsam upon the trees, a general indication of good land. The Tuskets are either lakes or deep low streams, for a great part of their length, although they have many rapid places. The land is very good for roads being mostly dry, and not very stony. Between the 21st and 27th September there is very little land fit for cultivation S. of the Digby township line. N. of the line for 2 miles I should suppose that about ¼ of the land is fit for cultivation. We observed that the land there was best within 3 or 4 miles of the salt water.

From the accounts we received from different persons, I conclude that there is plenty of iron ore near the Moose River. The highland called the South Mountain is everywhere full of rocks of granite: and is probably made by solid hills of that kind of rock, covered a few feet deep, with earth and loose stones. As we descend towards the salt water, or Annapolis River, the stones change to slate, the coarse blue Porphyry common about Halifax, and another hard gritty kind of stone. Just where we get below the layer of granite is the place where the iron ore appears. August 30th and October 3rd and 4th there is good land enough in one body adjoining the Liverpool road, west of the Nictaw and S. of the Annapolis township line for 250 farms. Near this upon the head streams of the Nictaw and Wild Cat River (Sept 1st and 2nd) there is I should think enough for 100. The land for 4 miles N. of the Nictaw and 7 miles S. of Annapolis river (Oct. 3rd, 4th, and 5th) is I believe chiefly good: but I believe it is chiefly granted, although not much of it is settled. Octr. 8th we passed a piece of very good land. I think it probably contains 4000 acres, this if not too far from the road must be worth settling. Not far from the S. end of the lake, which this lies by the side of, we had passed a very good hardwood hill on the 27th of August.

There are 4 or 5000 acres of good land by the side of the lakes, which we struck of the 9th of October and on the streams which fall into and run out of them, there may also be near 1000 acres of good upland about the lake which we struck on the 10th and there is a considerable quantity of good alder swamp near to this land, but it would not be possible to make a road from it on our track to Windsor or

Falmouth at any reasonable expense as the land is all mountainous the best access to this land is from Horton.

There are about 2000 acres of land fit for cultivation at the head of the branch of Pissaquid River which we examined Oct. 14th, 15th, and 16th, laying in a compact body and there is considerable more near it to the southward and westward in insulated pieces, surrounded by barrens: a good road might be made without a great expense by following the river. There is probably a considerable quantity of good land on the streams of La Have and Port Midway, between the places where we crossed them on our second and third courses. The northern half of the township of Chester is more absolutely barren than any place near it, being wholly mountainous hills of granite, except perhaps, a little piece at the N.E. corner. The soil almost throughout the whole of the western part of the province is gravelly although the gravel varies according to the kind of stone which lies upon the land. It varies also greatly in fertility according to the different proportions and qualities of the vegetable mould which is everywhere mixed with it. The most barren gravel is that which is chiefly composed of slate, or that which contains a large quantity of isinglass. This last kind of the common soil of upland near Shelburne--it seems to be chiefly formed by the decayed granite which is there very full of isinglass. We have not met with any other place which was extremely poor, where the rocks were of the granite kind, except it was rendered barren by being almost all stone.

The stones between the two Rivers of Chester (July 15th) and from the station of July 15th to July 22nd are a mixture of slate and the blue mountain stone. The slate contains a great deal of sulphurous iron pyrites and is consequently of an iron rusty color on the outside. The water in the brooks and swamps is of a very dark color, and very frequently lets fall a quantity of Ochre in places where there is no current.

In many places the soil of this land is loamy from a mixture of decayed slate, which resembles clay, mixed with the gravel, but this kind of loam is far from being fertile soil, being always impregnated with iron vitriol. Very near the coast there are some hills of a better kind, the soil of which has a mixture of real clay. From the station of July 22nd to 27th and for 4 miles farther west, the stones are wholly the coarse porphyry, which I have called the blue mountain stone. The soil is chiefly a gravel of the same kind of stone, and very poor. Above half this distance is covered with swamps (see G. O. No. 5) which are filled with a coarse kind of mud, very barren in its present state. From the last mentioned station to August the 7th the stones are chiefly the coarse white granite, with a small proportion of porphyry and of a much coarser grain than at Halifax containing isinglass. There are also a few large rocks of another kind of granite very rough and coarse, of a dull reddish brown color. From August 7th to 10th the stones are the common porphyry. We here saw very little earth of any kind, except swamp mud. From August 10th to 15th the stones are chiefly slate, which is apparently free from sulphur ore, and which consequently does not render the land barren. The soil here is in many places somewhat loamy, from a mixture of decayed slate. Upon the Tuskets, and from the 10th to the 22nd of September the stone is chiefly the common porphyry with some slate in most places. Much of the poorest part of this land, has in the soil a considerable mixture of that kind of loam which is made from decayed slate, but the common soil is gravel.

Within 3 or 4 miles of Annapolis Basin and River slate and porphyry are commonly to be found. The soil for half a mile breadth along Annapolis basin is sand. This is the only place in the western part of the province where we have seen a soil wholly sandy, although many pine hills near Shelburne and other places have a considerable mixture of sand with the gravel.

There is clay in most places near the sea shore and near the Annapolis River but we have never seen any at the distance of 3 miles from the salt water or the Annapolis River, except upon the Nictaw, where perhaps it may be found 5 miles from that river. We saw no clay at Shelburne or Tusket. The hardwood land near the Nictaw, has a loamy soil, made by a mixture of clay, there is also a very small portion of clay mixed in the soil of the tops of some of the hills in the spruce lands which lie N. of Margarets' Bay. Except the above we have not seen any place but what had a gravelly pit.

The marsh at Windsor has a reddish clayey soil certainly not made from the wash of the hills which have no such soil nor does is resemble the soil of the salt marshes at New York and other places which I have seen, where it is a blue mud.

I think it is, in a great measure made from decayed limestone and plaister, which are to be found everywhere in the lowland near the marsh, and of which it is probable there is an abundance in the bad of the basin of Mines. The limestone in the bank of the Windsor River (Pissaquid River) changes as it decays, into a reddish brown kind of marl which when mixed with an equal quantity of light coloured earth, is of the same color as the soil of the marshes. This kind of limestone decays fast where it is exposed to the air. I observed the bones of a man laying on the beach in a place where the bank is a solid rock of limestone, with 3 or 4 feet of earth upon it. On mentioning this to some people at Windsor, I was told here was an old French burying ground and that three lengths of graves had been washed away within 20 years the earth falling down the bank as fast as the limestone, by which is supported, decayed.

FINAL REPORT

May it please Your Excellency

The Committee which Your Excellency has been pleased to appoint to take the subject of the culture of Hemp in this Province into consideration, having deliberated on the means, beg leave to report,

That it is their united opinions which they derive from the individual knowledge of some of the members of your committee, and the very positive statements of other persons whom they have consulted on the occasion, that there are large tracts of country, now under culture, on which this article may be produced to advantage, if the means which your committee propose to recommend to Your attention are adopted;- but, as it is an article which the farmers, in general, have been unaccustomed to, there is, at present, very little seed in the Province; and, at this time, it is too late, in the season, to procure it. Your committee, therefore, have in contemplation the promotion of this object in future; and they think the season of 1802 may, with exertion, produce some consequences; - but it is to a progressive attention on which the hopes of an extensive supply must be grounded, - First from those lands which are known to everyone who has travelled through the country - and Secondly from those which have been explored by individuals who have reported what they have seen in the more distant wilderness.

The first of these your committee will reserve for a future report; in regard to the second, as Your Excellency has not confined us to any particular line, but has left us without limitation in the pursuit of the object, we presume to lay before you a plan from which we derive great hopes that the expectations of Government will ultimately be answered, to a considerable extent, and the Province, at the same time, be essentially benefited.

It must be well known to Your Excellency, who has traversed this peninsula in various directions, that it is everywhere intersected by considerable rivers and their various branches, and that lakes of every gradation, from a few acres to a day's journey in length, are numberless. You must have perceived, wherever you have been, that these rivers and lakes, especially the former are usually bounded by interval lands, and marshes which are formed of the richest soil. - The testimony of the Indians, Acadians and others agree in stating these spots to be more extensive and better in quality - abounding more in finer timber, the further they recede from the sea coast, with which, except at the Isthmus of Cumberland, this peninsula is surrounded.

Your committee deem it an object of great importance, that Government should be put in possession of facts, and no longer rely on vague reports which, on one hand, have often depressed the worth of this country below its real value;- whilst others, especially the French writers, have given flattering descriptions above the truth. To this end we recommend that a survey shall be taken, of a nature as extensive as the season, to the end of October, will admit, of those inland parts which have been least visited or are entirely unknown, with the view of discovering those spots which are best adapted to the growth of Hemp, and the furnishing of other naval stores. We presume that if it is in the contemplation of Government or the Legislature ever to promote a more accurate survey of the Province, such a previous tour as the one now proposed, will greatly forward it by directing the more minute attention of the surveyors to the most interesting objects; and, thereby, save much time, trouble and expense.

We, also, flatter ourselves that much of the advantageous side of the character of Nova
Scotia will prove to be well founded. In that case, we hope Government may deem it both for the interest of the mother

country and this Province, to encourage the settlement of those lands, by means of the numerous loyal emigrants, particularly the Hollanders, who have no immediate settlements or occupations in England. Your Committee beg leave to point out the rich marsh lands of Cumberland and the Bason-of-Mines, well known to Your Excellency, so exactly similar to those of Holland, and which are of such vast extent, as to promise to become, under the approbation and protection of Government, in the highest degree, worthy the attention of those people.

Mich. Wallace.
J G Pyke
Jonathan Tremain
Law. Hartsborne
William Sabatier
George J. Parkyns.

Halifax
May 5th, 1801.

To His Excellency Sir John Wentworth Bart.

&ca. &ca. &ca.

THE MAGAZINE

OF

NATURAL HISTORY.

DECEMBER, 1835.

ORIGINAL COMMUNICATIONS.

ART. I. [*Conclusions on the Results on the Vegetation of Nova Scotia, and on Vegetation in general, and on Man in general, of certain Natural and Artificial Causes deemed to actuate and affect them.* By Mr. TITUS SMITH. Communicated by R. G.

R. G. sent the following dissertation, as cut from a colonial paper, and, with it, information that " it has not appeared in any other publication," and that the author of it " is a person of confessedly great and original talent; one who has been almost entirely self-taught in every branch of knowledge with which he is acquainted; and " that " his original genius, and his acquisitions, have been the means of introducing him to the correspondence of Dr. Grey of Edinburgh, and other persons of scientific pursuits."

The dissertation in the printed copy is headed, " Natural History of Nova Scotia; " and this heading is followed by this preface: — " The following Paper was read by Mr. Titus Smith, the Philosopher of the Dutch Village, before the Halifax Mechanics' Institute, on Wednesday evening, the 14th January. It abounds with original views, minute and curious information, and furnishes additional evidence of the richness of those stores which a life of observation and reflection has accumulated in a naturally powerful mind."]

SOME knowledge of the vegetable productions of the earth is necessary to every man. But, to the man who cultivates the soil, it must be particularly useful to learn the means by which its fertility is preserved or increased in those situations where the hand of man has never disturbed the operations of nature. It is found, by long experience in America, that woodland, when first cleared, will yield a succession of good

THE MAGAZINE OF NATURAL HISTORY.

DECEMBER, 1835.

ORIGINAL COMMUNICATIONS.

[Art. I. Conclusions on the Results on the Vegetation of Nova Scotia, and on Vegetation in general, and on Man in general, of certain Natural and Artificial Causes deemed to actuate and affect them. By Mr. Titus Smith. Communicated by R. G.

R. G. sent the following dissertation, as cut from a colonial paper, and, with it, information that "it has not appeared in any other publication," and that the author of it " is a person of confessedly great and original talent; one who has been almost entirely self-taught in every branch of knowledge with which he is acquainted; and" that "his original genius, and his acquisitions, have been the means of introducing him to the correspondence of Dr. Grey of Edinburgh, and other persons of scientific pursuits."

The dissertation in the printed copy is headed, "Natural History of Nova Scotia;" and this heading is followed by this preface: — "The following Paper was read by Mr. Titus Smith, the Philosopher of the Dutch Village, before the Halifax Mechanics' Institute, on Wednesday evening, the 14th January. It abounds with original views, minute and curious information, and furnishes additional evidence of the richness of those stores which a life of observation and reflection has accumulated in a naturally powerful mind."]

Some knowledge of the vegetable productions of the earth is necessary to every man. But, to the man who cultivates the soil, it must be particularly useful to learn the means by which its fertility is preserved or increased in those situations where the hand of man has never disturbed the operations of nature. It is found, by long experience in America, that woodland, when first cleared, will yield a succession of good crops for six or seven years, or, if cleared without much burning, for a longer period; but that it finally " runs out" (to use a common expression), and requires a hundred loads of manure to the acre to make it produce, for three years, as good crops as it did when new. But should it be pastured, the soil, if not originally very fertile, appears slowly to become more barren for thirty or forty years: yet, if bushes should be allowed to overrun this worn-out ground, it will, upon cutting them down, be found to have improved in proportion to the time it has been covered by them.

It appears, therefore, to be necessary to the preservation of the fertility of the earth, that it should be covered entirely with a coat of vegetation, since, from the time that a growth of young wood springs up, till the forest has reached its full size, the ground that it covers is becoming every day more fertile; but when the wood is destroyed, and prevented from returning by the pasturage of cattle, it is for many years constantly becoming more barren. The cause of this deterioration of the soil will be readily conceived, by reflecting that those elements which distinguish a fertile soil easily assume an aerial form, and that they are in that state absorbed by the leaves of plants, and, where these have been in a great measure destroyed by pasturage, are borne by the winds to those situations where they are arrested by a luxuriant vegetation. As we must observe, then, that the soil, so frequently impoverished when managed by man, always retains its fertility in a state of nature, it must be important to the agriculturist to attend to the operations of the great Cultivator. For, rough and rude as our forests appear, they form a portion of the "garden of God." In all their various productions, there is nothing superfluous or out of place.

The student of natural history in America possesses some advantages over the inhabitants of its mother country. He has under his eye tracts where the works of nature have not been disturbed by man. In Europe, some persons of great knowledge appear still to doubt whether there ever was a period in which the land generally presented the appearance of a forest, and whether the soil of peat bogs is formed from decayed vegetables. Strange as these doubts must appear to any person of observation brought up in the woods of America, still it is curious to observe the operations of nature in preserving forest, and in forming this "savings' bank," this reserve of fuel for the use of man, destined for his supply when he shall, by his negligence, have destroyed the forest wood.

Nearly all this province has, it is certain, at no very distant period, been covered with wood; not excepting the granite hills, which have little or no earth upon them. Upon the fertile soils the vegetation is composed of hardwood (trees with deciduous leaves), and succulent plants with annual leaves. Their growth is rapid, and the outer bark (technically called the epidermis, the only part of a tree that is very durable) is extremely thin. The annual crop of leaves, the trees overthrown by the autumnal storms, or dying of age, and the lowest twigs, which are constantly perishing by suffocation, furnish a large quantity of dead vegetable matter, which, by the operations of the Fungi, insects, and the succeeding process of putrefaction, is soon changed into mould, which must continue to accumulate till the trees are fully grown; thus preparing a soil for the cultivator, by removing to the surface the most fertile part, from the greatest depth to which the roots of a tree can reach. Upon this soil neither turf nor peat earth is formed; but a fine mould lies under the dead leaves. This portion of the forest can rarely be affected by fires in the woods, as the leaves in summer are full of watery juices. Should a part of it (as sometimes happens) be overthrown by a hurricane, it is very soon replaced. Shoots from the old roots and seedlings spring up, among which a few scattered plants of the balsam fir [Abies balsamifera Mx.] appear, which, overtopping the hardwood, by their shelter accelerate its growth, and, being short-lived trees, are, in their turn, overtopped and suffocated by the hardwood, when it no longer needs their assistance.

Upon a barren soil the trees are generally of the fir kind, all evergreens, except the hacmetac [Larix pendula Lamb, or else microcarpa Lamb]: the greater part of the shrubs and plants are also evergreens. Their leaves contain more resinous and more woody matter, than the plants of fertile soils; they have also a strong thick epidermis. The trees on this soil grow slowly, and have an appearance which is called "scrubbed:" this is partly caused by the unusual quantity of the epidermis, which increases in an inverse proportion to the growth of the tree (a black spruce [Abies nigra H. K.] with a very rough scaly bark being sometimes a hundred years old, when not more than 4 in. in diameter); and partly by a large quantity of resin, which flows from the knots produced by the dying of the lower branches, and from wounds made in the bark by insects; as the wood of these trees is much more solid and resinous than that of the same species in situations where it grows rapidly.

In addition to the turpentines of the fir tribe, the wax of the candleberry myrtle [Myrica sp.], and the oily substance on the buds of the Dutch myrtle and the alder, many of the leaves of the plants of barren soils contain a considerable quantity of resinous matter.

The large proportion of these two almost imperishable substances, resin, and the epidermis of trees and other vegetables, appears to be connected with the formation of turf; as it is certain that they are produced in the greatest abundance on the most barren soils, and that in the same situations the greatest quantity of turf is formed. It may also be remarked that there are, in the vegetables of the most barren soils, very large proportions of tannin and gallic acid, well known to be very powerful in resisting putrefaction. The leaves of the kalmia [six species, and some varieties, are known to botanists: the species are all natives of North

America] and uva ursi [Arctostaphylos Uva ursi], and the bark and seed cones of the spruces [certain species of Abies], contain them in abundance.

Leather may be tanned with the leaves of the kalmia; those of the uva ursi are the principal tanning material used in the north of Europe. The cones of the black spruce appear to the taste as astringent as gall nuts. The taste of these powerful antiseptics is not very perceptible in the scales of epidermis that are perpetually falling as the trees increase in growth; but it is probable that they are contained in them in a state of combination with some other substances[15], and that they assist in giving them their uncommon durability.

When the woods of fir become so thick that the kalmia perishes, the soil generally becomes covered with various kinds of dry moss. As this is a vegetable which is not quickly decomposed, it forms a portion of the turf, which is connected by its roots; and it assists in preventing its decomposition by excluding the light and external air; and securing it from being affected by sudden changes in the temperature of the atmosphere; for which purposes it is very suitable; being a bad conductor of heat, as may be proved by the late period at which ground covered with it freezes in winter and thaws in spring.

Although many other necessary consequences of these facts would suggest themselves to the minds of those who are versed in chemistry, enough, perhaps, has been said to give some idea of the causes which prevent the rapid change of dead vegetable matter to mould upon barren soils. At any rate, the fact is certain, that a turf is formed, the depth of

---

[15] Probably oxygen, for which astringents have so much affinity, that an infusion of galls will precipitate silver from its solution in a [an omission here] form.

---

which, in an old[16] [? forest, is] generally in direct proportion to the barrenness of the subsoil. Its utility is obvious, as it produces [? thickets of] timber, which grows to a size fit for many useful purposes upon the barren whinstone plains, where the [? surface is] covered by from 1 ft. to 2 ft. of broken stone [? and upon] hills of granite which have not 4 in. of [? any sort of] soil. It also increases the earthy portion of the [? turf, ? soil] by slowly decomposing the surface of the subjacent rock. I have seen a growth of tall black spruce, about two hundred years old, upon a piece of ground composed of broken whinstone, and rounded pebbles and gravel, mixed with so very small a proportion of earth, that it must, in a dry season, have been impossible for any tree to have lived upon it had it been deprived of its covering of turf, which was about 15 in. thick; yet, by the means of this layer, it was enabled to produce useful timber, some of which was 18 in. in diameter.

This turf appears to the eye to contain considerable proportions of decayed wood, little changed from the state to which it was reduced by the fungi, and of the epidermis of trees and shrubs, and the cones of spruce very little altered. At the bottom, a very shallow layer, generally mixed with charcoal, approaches to the state of mould. In this bottom layer the seeds of the raspberry [Rubus idaeus L. is wild in North America; and several other species are too] are to be found in abundance, with [? some f of those of the wild cherry, red-berried elder [Sambucus pubens Mx.], [? another] shrubs that usually spring up after a fire. The [? seeds of] the pigeon berry, and several other plants, may [? be found] occasionally in every part of the turf in [? a dormant] state.

Woods of the fir kind are much exposed [? to fire]. In a dry season, the moss which covers the surface will burn like tow,

[16][The terminal part of this line, and of the next several lines, in the copy from which this is printed, is torn off.]

and soon communicates the fire to dry branches that produce [? a sufficient] flame to reach the green leaves above them, [? that acts] especially upon the spruce [Abies sp.] and balsam [Abies balsamifera Mx.], ? which are] more inflammable in a green state than [? when dry]. As they contain a considerable quantity of [? resinous] juices, and extinguish coals when thrown [? upon] them, it is probable that the property they [? possess], of producing an extraordinary quantity of [? flame, is] connected with the unusual proportion of [? resinous] fluids which they evolve during combustion, [? as the] remarkable crackling, and immense volume of smoke, produced by a fire in a thicket [? of black] spruce, have sometimes been mistaken for [? some kind of] storm, by persons at a distance of a mile [? from the] fire.

By these fires, the leaves and small spray [? of the, ? and the] branches are consumed, together with the [? coat of] litter which covered the surface, and which, by excluding the sunbeams, had kept the turf at a low and equal temperature.

The naked black surface is now exposed to the sun, and the process of putrefaction commences in earnest, affecting the turf as well as the roots of the vegetables which have been killed by the fire. The increased temperature of this natural hot-bed brings into action the vegetative powers of seeds which had lain dormant for centuries; raspberries spring up in abundance, together with red-berried elder, bird cherry, sumach, prickly alalia [? Aralia spinosa], and evergreen fumitory. The French willow [Epilobium augustifolium L.; or some one or more other species] and the cacalias, whose suffocating down is so troublesome to the thresher upon new lands, soon find out their favourite light soil. The whole face of the country is changed. Tracts of a hundred acres are thickly covered by raspberries, loaded with a luxuriant crop. The low barren levels overspread with blueberries; and large tracts occupied by the French willow, which forms so striking an object, with its long spikes of purplish red flowers; together with the large clusters of the scarlet elderberry, which appears occasionally in the low stony ground ; altogether give an idea of fertility which forms a remarkable contrast with the sterile appearance of the same soil previous to the fire.

Within three years this fertility disappears; the turf is greatly reduced in quantity; the land becomes hard and cold, presenting that exhausted appearance which always follows the raising of crops on a burnt soil. A few clumps only of the raspberry and French willow remain, in situations where the lightness of the soil is preserved by having the surface covered with broken stones, or the tops of fallen trees. Shoots from the white maple [Acer dasycarpon Ehrh. (syn., eriocarpon Mx.)] (the roots of which are never killed by fires), brakes, sweet fern [Comptonia aspleniifolia H. K.], dwarf willows, and withrod, occupy the ground, presently followed by alder; and, when they have formed a sufficient shelter, the firs again spring up, mixed with white birch [Betula opulifblia H. K.: see the Penny Cyclopedia] and poplars [several species inhabit North America]. In the lower and more barren tracts the blueberry [? Vaccinium ? venustum H. K.'] is, by degrees, overgrown by the kalmia and rhodora (Rhodora canadensis L.) which are, after the lapse of a few years, in their turn overtopped by the alder, which is always soon followed by a growth of firs. A number of plants whose seeds never vegetate during the fertile period now appear; among which we notice the mayflower, the trailing evergreens (lycopodiums), snakeroot [Aristolochia Seqientaria £..], mitchella [Mitchella repens W.], linnea [Linnae aborealis Gron.: the American form of this species is different from the European one], pigeon berry, mountain tea [Gaultheria procumbens L.], maidenhair [Adiantum pedatum L.], several kinds of aster, and golden rods [Solidago]. The mosses follow, and the thicket, in the course of thirty or forty years, resumes nearly its former appearance, except that the trees are smaller, and that the balsam fir forms a larger proportion of the wood. This tree of rapid growth, by its shelter, covers the more valuable spruce from winds, and prevents it from forming strong lateral branches, which would deteriorate the timber, till, having reached the height of 30 ft. or 40 ft., it is overtopped and suffocated by it. When a very old growth of hemlock [Abies canadensis Mx.] and spruce has been destroyed by fire, it sometimes happens that a growth of beech [Fagus sylvatica L. and ferruginea L. are wild in North America], birch, and maple takes its place. It also sometimes happens that when an old grove of pine is destroyed, it is replaced by white [Betula populifolia H. K.] and yellow birch [Betula excelsa H. K.: see the Penny Cyclopaedia], and oak. But these changes are less frequent than is imagined. Most hemlock woods, when killed by fires, are at first overgrown with birch hooppoles, mixed with firs; but, when the birch has reached the height of 20 ft. or 30 ft., it turns mossy, and continues nearly stationary for perhaps twenty years, during which a young growth of hemlock again springs up, and most of the birches perish. In a similar way, the pine woods, when killed, are first covered with alder, followed by white birch [Betula populifolia H. K.], poplars, and a little oak; but these trees rarely reach any considerable size before they are overtopped by spruce and hacmetac, which is, finally, again mixed with pine. Whenever a growth of hardwood, on a poor soil, is cut down, the land burnt over, and exposed for several years to the pasturage of cattle, it will, if left undisturbed, grow up with a mixture of fir and spruce.

Wherever the soil is so poor that turf is formed on the upland, peat earth is formed in the swamps and bogs. It is most abundant on vitriolic soils, and, generally, in situations that have formerly been ponds or shallow lakes: most of the trees that grow on their banks fall, finally, into them. Every kind of wood sinks after remaining a certain time in the water. The leaves constantly falling in are never returned to the land. Vegetable substances embedded in mud, under water, are remarkably durable. I have taken up a stick of white birch from a beaver pond, which, from the growth of wood on the site of the house, I judged, must have been embedded for near a century. Neither the bark nor the wood was distinguishable from those of a green tree. Yet the inner bark of this tree decays in one summer when exposed to the air. Heavy rains, which send torrents of water into the swamps, make a small addition to the material of the bogs; but it is but a small one while the forest is growing. On a barren soil, the surface is entirely covered with a rough coat of vegetation. Even where the spruce is so thick as to suffocate the shrubs and perennial plants, the ground is covered with a fleece of dry moss, which, like a strainer, retains every thing that can form turf. The brooks on this soil, however rapid they may be, have low banks, and are hardly perceived to wear away any portion of the earth. They run upon beds of stones, which are themselves prevented from attrition by the water moss and byssus which cover them; the dead leaves, twigs, and scales of bark, which fall into the streams, do not go far before they are arrested by the fallen trees which cross the brooks, forming little patches of swamp where the banks are low. But it is after every fire that runs through the woods, that large additions are made to the deposits of peat earth. Very extensive fires in the woods are so generally followed by heavy floods of rain, that there is some reason to think that the enormous pillars of smoke have some share in producing them. The water now rushes over a surface smoothed by the fire, and carries with it into the swamps and ponds considerable quantities of charcoal, fragments of turf, spruce cones, pieces of the outer bark of trees and shrubs, and other light substances; among which the shining shells of coleopterous insects are very perceptible, in quantities fully sufficient to account for the ammonia which is yielded by pit coal, if coal is formed, as seems probable, from antediluvian deposits of vegetable matter. The mud accumulated in lakes and ponds is prevented from passing into the sea by aquatic plants. The bottoms of muddy lakes have a thick growth of water grass wherever the water is about 6 ft. in depth; the shallows are occupied by water lilies [nine species inhabit North America], Sagittaria, and other plants, among which the Pontederia, which produces such large spikes of blue flowers, is the most remarkable.

The byssus (the green slimy plant that is so common in fresh water in the hot season), entangled among the stems of these plants when the water is high, and drying as it falls, forms a considerable quantity of paper, like that from which the hornet makes his nest; a substance which I have observed to form a large proportion of peat from Ireland, taken from a part of the bog where it had formerly been dug out, and which had again filled up. When the lake or pond is so far filled up, that the mud is nearly bare in a dry season, the Andromeda calyculata is the first shrub that grows upon it; bog moss with Indian cups follows, and the Indian tea, rosemary leaved kalmia [Kalmia glauca L. var. rosmarinifolia Ph.], Dutch myrtle, and other bog plants and shrubs, coming in, with a sprinkling of the tough-rooted cotton grasses and sedges, a strong turf is formed, which alternately floats on the water or rests on the mud, according to the moisture or dryness of the season. Many considerable marshes of this description may be found by the sides of lakes which rise with every flood, with the exception of a few spots occupied by small clumps of firs, which will be found, upon removing the moss, to be the sites of old beaver houses. In the great barren plain, in the western part of the province, there are morasses of this description several miles in extent, producing only bog plants and shrubs of a small size, where, in a wet season, the weary traveller sinks, at every step, a foot deep in water, in consequence of the bending of the blanket of mossy turf upon which he is walking; and which he can, at pleasure, shake for 30 ft. around, manifestly perceiving the undulation of the water beneath him. It appears to be necessary to the preservation of peat, that it should be always nearly covered with water. When the water sinks below its surface, as it generally does in dry weather, in swamps which have large streams running through them, the upper layer changes to a kind of mould capable of producing grass and alder, and the swamps become natural meadows, which are mostly of a poor quality on stony vitriolic soils, but better where the upland is a sandy loam, because a portion of it is always carried by rains into the swamps; while on the rocky soils scarcely any earth is mixed with the vegetable matter. The principal collections of peat earth are at the sources of small streams: some water always runs from them; but many of them have no streams which enter them but such as fail in dry weather. These deposits on granite soils are generally collected in basins formed by the rock; but on the vitriolic soils, where the peat is most abundant, and of the best quality, the soil is rendered impervious to water by slate clay mixed with ochre. The wet peat having the property of changing the slate to clay, considerable quantities of vitriol are contained in the water which enters peat bogs; but it is immediately decomposed. Ochre is always deposited where a rill of vitriolic water enters the swamps: the sulphur probably unites with the peat, as the water runs from the swamp soft and free from vitriol, but usually holding a little carbonaceous matter in solution.

As more vitriol is formed on open ground than there could have been when it was covered with wood, it is probable that the peat earth of our bogs is in a different state from that of Europe. We see here that, when the land has been cleared for a number of years, the water runs clear from a swamp, sometimes on granite, and often on slate and whinstone soils; while, in the woods, it is generally brown, except it has passed over limestone. However, in the state in which it is, our peat makes good fuel, and could by many be procured cheaper than wood, did it not interfere with the business of the summer season.

It is worthy of remark that, in tropical climates, no peat earth is formed; the heat causing dead vegetable matter to go through the process of putrefaction in every situation, and, of course, generating great quantities of hydrogen and carbonic acid gas from the same materials that are slowly forming a bituminous fuel in our peat bogs; and, it is probably owing to this circumstance that swampy situations are very unhealthy in those climates; while, in the regions where the severity of the winters makes a greater supply of fuel necessary, the half-decomposed vegetable matter is preserved in a state that prevents it from undergoing the putrefactive process, much to the advantage of its inhabitants; for it is well known that there are no countries more healthy, nor any which furnish greater supplies of hardy men to more fertile and less salubrious regions, than those which abound in bogs of peat earth. When a wood of firs is killed by fire, in the course of a few years most of the trees fall to the ground. If these are consumed by a second fire, the ground becomes so bare that firs will not live upon it in exposed situations. But the swamps, which escape the effects of the fire always, together with the different species of fir, contain alder. This shrub, producing abundance of light seed, which is spread far and wide by the winds, usually composes the greater part of the first growth upon bleak naked hills, especially upon those that have not more than 3 in. or 4 in. of earth above their rocky basis. When the shrubbery of alder attains the height of 3 ft. or 4 ft., the firs always begin to appear. All the trees of the fir kind, it should be observed, are, as well as the alder, furnished with winged seeds, which fit them for being borne by winds as far as is necessary to cover the intervals between swamps. Thus, it appears that the swamps are the seed-beds from which the land is again sowed with firs as often as they are destroyed by fires; and, also, with alder, whenever its shelter is needed to cover the firs.

This process of nature was favoured by the habits of the Indians, who carefully avoided setting the woods on fire. But the great influx of inhabitants in 1783 produced, in the course of a few years, a complete change in the appearance of the forest. A great number of new settlements were formed. The fires necessary for clearing the land were communicated to the spruce thickets, and spread frequently as far as they extended. The profusion of herbage which followed the fire, for a time furnished a pasture for the cattle. This failed in three or four years. The next dry season the fire was rekindled, for the purpose of renewing it, which it would do in a less degree. Raspberries, French willow, and other vegetables, would appear upon part of the ground, but of inferior growth. The roots of the spruces and balsam fir spread horizontally, and take but slight hold of the ground. Being loosened by the sinking of the turf, they are overthrown by every wind, and furnish fuel for successive fires, which are usually rekindled every dry season by design or negligence, till, the combustible matter being consumed, with the exception of that portion which is washed by rains into the swamps, the ground becomes so much exhausted, that it produces only a growth of heathy shrubs, among which the kalmia predominates; and, in many places, it is necessary that this should continue long enough to form a few inches of turf, before the alder and other large shrubs can be reproduced, as a shelter for another growth of firs.

Near to the cultivated districts, the wood, in time, becomes scarce; and the swamps are finally attacked by the axe; thus destroying the trees which used to furnish seeds to the ground where fires had destroyed the wood: and it is probable that, at no very distant period, many large tracts will present nearly the same appearance as the naked heaths and downs of the old world.

Although the kalmia burns freely in a dry season, it does not seem possible to destroy it by fires where the surface is covered with broken stones. After it is burnt off, a growth of whortles [Vaccinium sp.] often springs up, and bears a plentiful crop for two or three years; but it is finally overpowered by shoots from the roots of the kalmia. It disappears, however, in some situations, where the turf is completely burnt off from sand or gravel, and is replaced by a growth of lower or trailing shrubs, which more completely exclude the light and air from the exhausted soil. These are the uva ursi, the crakeberry heath [Empetrum nigrum L.], the yellow-flowering cistus [Hudsdonia ericoides L.], the ceratiola, or Acadian heath [Ceratiola ericoides L.], and (near the sea) the Acadian savine. Upon comparing what we observe upon our barren lands with the productions of similar soils in Europe, we shall find reason to believe that the heaths and downs of the old country have formerly been forests; and that they might again be covered with wood, without any great expense, by imitating the process by which the forest is reproduced on our barrens. It would, for this purpose, be necessary to form such seed-beds as our swamps are, and theirs must have been, at suitable distances, by planting in, and on the edges of, bogs and wet moors, clumps composed of all the trees and shrubs naturally growing in the country ; to which it would be necessary to add a sprinkling of such plants as are natives of the woodlands, many of which are necessary to the success of the forest, either as a shelter for seedlings, or for other useful purposes.

The principal trees of our forests are, the white and red pines [the white is Pinus Strobus L., the red is Pinus resinosa H. K.], the spruces [Abies alba H. K, rubra Lamb., nigra H. K., and perhaps other species], hemlock [Abies canadensis H.K., beech, sugar maple [Acer saccharinum L.: sugar is procured in North America from other species besides], grey oak [Quercus ?ambigua Mx.], yellow birch, and white ash [Fraxinus americana L.]. The elms, and the large black cherry, common forest trees farther southward, are here nearly confined to alluvial soils. Most of the smaller trees, and many shrubs, are necessary to introduce these upon open land, as they will not succeed unless sheltered when young. Two of these sheltering trees, the red-flowering maple [Afcer rubrum Ehrh.] and the balsam fir, extend their protection to all, as they are to be found upon every kind of soil. The fir is a tree of rapid growth; and the roots of the maple are never injured when the stem is killed by fires, or cut down; and, consequently, always throw out a number of shoots, which, in the course of one summer, after a fire, form clumps of shrubbery 3 ft. or 4 ft. in height. The white birch and the poplars, always with a mixture of fir and maple, and often of oak and spruce, form the shelter of the white pine. The hemlock is sheltered by the yellow birch, mixed with fir, spruce, and maple; and these young groves of birch, and all other groves of young hardwood, are protected on the open side, if such there should be, by a thick belt of firs. Wherever, also, the edge of an old grove of beech or fir is exposed, by the destruction of the wood on the adjoining barren, a very thick belt of fir springs up; which, in the course of a few years, completely shelters it from the wind and sun. The red larch, or hacmetac [Pursh has given Pinus pendula, now iarix pendula Lamb., as the "hacmatack;" and Larix microcarpa Lamb, is given, in one work, as the red larch], forms a portion of the shelter for black spruce on rocky barrens. The alder, mixed with withrod, dwarf willows, and shoots from the roots of the red-flowering maple, serves to shelter the white birch, poplar, spruce, fir, and hacmetac. The seedling plants of the alder require the shelter of the kalmia, or of the evergreen, and dead leaves of the common plants of poor land; the hawkweeds [Hieracium sp.], the goldenrods, the trailing evergreens, the Mitchells, &c. The kalmias, spiraeas, and rhodora [Rhoddra canadensis L.] have seeds so minute, that the young plants are scarcely visible to the naked eye, and perish in a few hours if exposed to sun or wind. They are sheltered by the mayflower and other plants. The rhodora (the shrub which produces such an abundance of red flowers in the spring) usually vegetates upon the roots of the horse fern, which it finally destroys. The tough creeping roots of the mountain tea serve to bind the rotten wood and the coarser parts of the turf, and prevent them from being displaced by frost. The creeping vines of the linnea cover broken stones, and preserve the moisture of the small portion of turf or soil beneath them. The lichens and mosses are necessary to the other plants of barren soils: their roots form a sward, and they prevent the ground from freezing early, or to a great depth, and from thawing easily when frozen; while naked patches of poor gravel freeze suddenly, and, thawing with every mild spell in winter, imbibe a great quantity of water, which is retained by the frozen subsoil, till, freezing again, by its increased volume it so shakes and overturns the ground, as to throw out the roots of small plants; and frequently kills the bark of the large by mechanical pressure.

Where the soil is extremely poor, it frequently happens that rocks elevated by the winter's frost and subsiding in spring, and other accidents, bring a portion of naked soil to the surface, upon which no common plant can live, as a seedling of one summer's growth would be so very small, that the roots would necessarily be thrown out of the ground by the frost. The lichen ericetorum is the vegetable which serves to heal these breaches in the green coating of the earth. This is a white scurfy crust, which, spreading over the naked soil, and shooting up little flesh-coloured tubercles that have the appearance of diminutive mushrooms, strikes its roots some depth into the earth, and forms a sward which prevents the water from easily entering, and secures the surface from being broken by the alternate frosts and thaws of winter. Upon this crust caribou [reindeer] moss, and other lichens spring up, soon followed by hawkweed, golden rod [Solidago], kalmia, and alder.

The ferns, with their very tough matted roots, are useful, in many places, to prevent the turf from breaking. When decayed leaves and lichens have slightly covered a rock or mass of broken stone, on the dark shaded side of a steep hill, a crop of green moss overspreads the shallow soil, presently followed by a growth of polypod, whose roots connect the whole so firmly, that the heaviest rains do not wash it away from the sides of steep hills. We often find it difficult to introduce grass into a drained swamp; the very light soil, being raised upon pillars of ice, throwing the roots out of the ground; but in these swamps, when in a state of nature, the firm matted roots of the sheep polypod and the horse fern are never moved. Some of the sedges, in the same situation, have roots nearly as strong as pack thread; and it has been found by experience, that the easiest mode of introducing clover and upland grasses into a drained swamp is, simply, to give it a dressing with stable manure as soon as it is drained, without breaking the natural turf of the swamp, which always prevents the frosts from moving the surface, long enough to allow the roots of the upland grasses to acquire their full growth. The family of lichens comprehends the crusts of various colours which overspread the rocks and stems of trees, the paper-like mosses, the white caribou moss, and the thread-like clusters of yellowish or black moss which hang from the branches of dead trees. Although they contain a considerable quantity of substance resembling starch, and a large proportion of carbonaceous matter, they appear to derive their nourishment from the air alone; for the largest species, the rock tripe, which our Indians use instead of barley for their soups, grows most frequently upon the perpendicular faces of ledges of rock. These vegetables, besides furnishing food for the caribou, or reindeer, and protecting trees and rocks from the effects of the weather, serve to introduce soil upon hills of naked rock. It is first overspread with the crustaceous species; these are followed by the leafy kinds: when they decay with age and crumble to pieces, their bulk is but little diminished. As soon as an inch of turf is formed, the caribou moss appears. A small portion of the rock is changed to sand by the action of the turf. The Acadian heath [Ceratiola mcoldes L.] and the Potentilla tridentata finally spring up, followed, as the turf increases, by black whortle, candleberry myrtle, and other shrubs. The small long-limbed Hudson's Bay pine [Pinus Banksiana Lamb.] is usually the first tree that grows on these shallow soils, which finally, if not prevented by fires, become capable of producing timber of a useful size.

The Fungi, those substances which we are accustomed to call mushrooms and touchwoods, are a family of vegetables which have a very different office: it is their business to assist in changing dead vegetable matter to mould or turf. Every dead vegetable; the trees overthrown by the wind; the leaves which fall annually; the low branches and underwood which die of suffocation, are immediately attacked by the Fungi, and soon reduced to an elementary state, in which they may serve again to become vegetables. Under their action the greater part of the vegetable disappears; the fungus occupies a considerable portion of the space which was once filled by the wood, not unfrequently the one half; and it is manifest, from the lightness of the remainder, that the greater part must have taken an aerial form. This decomposition is soon performed under the shade of woods, but much more slowly in open situations. A considerable part of the wood killed by fires continues sound till it falls, and is shaded by the plants that spring up near it; that is to say, dead vegetables are very quickly changed to aerial fluids only in those situations where there is a covering of foliage above them, which prevents the dissipation of their elements by absorbing them from the air. It seems probable, that the Fungi, the principal agents in decomposing dead vegetables, are, like the corals, formed by animalcula. [This view may not obtain any credit for the author of it, but is given here, that the discredit, as well as credit, due to him may be awarded to him.] The work they perform (an immense quantity) is analogous to that performed by insects. Like animal substances, some kinds of them are remarkably luminous when in a state of decay; and it appears to be to them that the phosphorescence of rotten wood is to be ascribed.

Some persons have considered it strange that our beech hills should so generally have the best soil near the top of the hill; that it should be of an inferior quality lower down; and that a barren spruce valley or plain should be found at the bottom; as it is certain that some dead leaves and decayed vegetables must be carried by streams of water into the valley, which can never return any to the hill. But, when we consider how often the barren land has had the growth upon it killed by fires, while the beech hill retained its foliage, we shall find reason to conclude that, in the first seasons after fires, while the ground was bare of plants, it must have returned, in an aerial state, to the green hills at least as much as it ever received from them.

When we consider the provision made for covering, immediately, every portion of naked ground with some kind of vegetables, which, by partly excluding the air and light, may prevent the too rapid decomposition and dissipation of the fertile principles of the soil, we shall find reason to doubt the utility of fallowing, especially upon shallow soils. That the practice is very ancient is certain; but it is also certain that man has, by mismanagement, impoverished some of the finest countries on earth. A green crop, cultivated with the hoe, will destroy weeds, and the eggs of insects, nearly as well as a fallow, without exposing the ground in a naked state for a whole season.

For a similar reason, it must be for the farmer's interest not to spread his manure over too much ground, but always to make his land rich enough to produce a crop that shall completely shade it. In a state of nature, the ground is always covered with a layer either of turf or vegetable mould. This would seem to point out to us that a top dressing is the proper mode of applying manure to grass, as it must, in that situation, preserve the heat and moisture of the ground more than it would if mixed with the soil. It ought always to be applied at the time when it will be very soon shaded by the grass. From experiments which I have tried, it appeared that it produced the greatest effect when spread at the time the trees began to unfold their leaves, and that there is a loss of one third upon that which is spread in the month of November. A top dressing, applied to plants in a garden when growing, is very useful: it is said to be the only way in which the land is manured in Japan ; and the population of the country seems to prove that the Japanese render the earth far more productive than any people in Europe. It appears to me to be the most economical method of applying manure, and that those skillful agricultural writers (certainly the majority) who disapprove of it have founded their opinion rather on theory than practice. But the fact, that earth does not confine aerial fluids, was for a long time nearly overlooked, nor was much attention paid to the portion of nourishment which plants receive through their leaves. When manure is ploughed into the ground, a part of it is changed, by putrefying, into an aerial state, and dissipated in the air before there are any leaves to arrest it. I have covered a small piece of ground with manure in December, and dug a part of it. The following spring the whole was sown with parsnips; the part which had been covered with manure through the winter produced a good crop; that which was dug in the fall was so poor, that the manure appeared to be thrown away. It may be useful to the agriculturist to reflect upon the haste with which nature covers every portion of naked ground with some kind of vegetables, which, by excluding the air and light, may prevent the decomposition and dissipation of the fertile principles of the soil. In those barren districts where the vegetation is exposed to be frequently destroyed by fire, the seeds are either furnished with a covering so firm that it can preserve the kernel uninjured for ages [p. 392.], or else fitted, by their minuteness, or their wing-like appendages, to be borne by winds to a considerable distance. We often find it very difficult to cultivate these vegetables, but cannot fail to observe that, in the "gardens of nature," seeds long buried in the soil, or annually strewed by winds over the surface for many years, without producing a single plant, will suddenly spring up [p. 392, 393.] and flourish, when, by one of those vicissitudes to which barren districts are exposed, a proper soil is prepared for them, and they are needed to cover the surface. When, by a long period of cultivation, the seeds of those plants which were the natural tenants of the soil have been destroyed, it is probable that this process could not be speedily renewed. Thus we find that, in those regions (once the site of flourishing nations) that have been depopulated by the necessary consequences of those vices that have hitherto always been introduced by the luxury that follows an immense accumulation of wealth, the fertility of the soil has disappeared with the cultivators. Ancient Syria and the neighbouring countries, we are informed by modern travellers, present such an appearance of sterility, that, were it not for the magnificent ruins that remain, it would be almost impossible to credit the accounts that historians have given of their population in former ages. A few small insulated spots remain as examples of their former fertility. The plains of Jericho and Hauran still produce "an hundred fold;" but the foot of man has not passed over what was once the kingdom of Idumea for ages. A few fishermen's huts are all that remain of ancient Tyre; and large districts, once thickly inhabited, present an appearance which seems to say, they will be cultivated no more. The discoveries of modern chemistry render it probable that a portion of the fertilising principles of the soil of these districts may have been removed to more highly cultivated regions, or to those which are still covered by forests, and are in a state of nature. While the once fertile territories which surround it have become deserts, Lebanon, it is well known, has literally become "a fruitful field," and more populous than any similar district in Europe; the mountainous situation having enabled the Druzes to preserve their liberty, and repel the rapacious Turk. If a country were cultivated for such a length of time, that the seeds of the plants which it produced when in a state of nature had all perished, and were then deserted by the cultivators, it must soon become very bare; for the weeds that flourish in cultivated ground require cultivation; and,when it ceased, would either perish or dwindle to a small size, not sufficient to supply the insects who [that] live upon plants. In such a state, it is certain that a portion of the fertile mould could, by the influence of the heat and light to which the surface was exposed, be changed into aerial fluids, which might be borne by winds to regions where they would be absorbed by the foliage of a forest or cultivated district. It is very probable that the unusual proportion of carbonic acid and hydrogen gases, which must be necessarily mixed in the common air where the soil is suddenly abandoned, may have had a share in increasing the malignity of those pestilential diseases, which have so often been observed to follow in the track of "desolating war."

Very large fertile districts have generally been found unhealthy; and it is doubtless necessary to the health of the whole animal creation, that the barren lands should bear to them that large proportion which is every where to be observed. The superior healthiness of the first occupiers of new land in America, has proved that the abundant foliage of a forest renders the air remarkably salubrious. Without entering into the minutiae of chemical detail, it may be observed, that it has been found that animals constantly emit from their lungs, and the surface of their bodies, an aerial fluid which is unfit for respiration ; that this aerial fluid is absorbed by the leaves of plants when exposed to light, and, being decomposed by their action, the part which rendered the air unwholesome to animals is retained, and serves to nourish the plant; while, at the same time, they emit the remainder in a state of pure perishable [respirable] air.

As a large proportion of the richest manure is quickly changed by putrefaction into noxious vapours, it is for the health of man that nothing which will serve to fertilise the soil should be neglected, and that cultivation should be pushed to the uttermost. It is also both for his health and his interest to preserve the forest, or to permit nature to reproduce it where it has been destroyed by fires, in those situations which are not required for cultivation or pasturage; since it is certain that uncultivated land, exposed to the sun continually, for a long time, becomes more barren, and that land overgrown with wood is for a long time slowly becoming more fertile.

Nature has strongly pointed out to man that he ought not to reside near to putrefying animal or vegetable substances. They are disgusting to his senses; most useful to him as manures. When he neglects his duty, other animals are provided to assist him. Large towns are usually overrun with dogs, most of which are kept for no other reason than the attachment felt by their owners for those humble, loving, and ever-faithful dependents. Were manure as carefully collected here as it is said to be in China and Japan, they might prove a nuisance; but here they are certainly useful. They live principally upon the offal in the streets and yards, and are well entitled to their living. With all our poverty, we have not heard of any person dying of hunger in Halifax; but there is good reason to believe that the removal of the dogs would cause numbers to die of pestilential diseases. The flies in our yards and houses have a similar employment. The effluvia of those substances, which taint the air, point out [to them those substances as] the proper nidus for their young, who [which], by speedily devouring them, in a great measure prevent their decomposition. These, in a few weeks, become flies, and enter our houses in swarms at the close of the hot season, when the air is more than at any other time charged with deleterious vapours. The motion of their wings performs, in our apartments, the same office that the winds do abroad, in preventing the separation of the different kinds of air: for it is well known that the noxious aerial fluids, which are most abundant, are either heavier, or much lighter, than common air; and were they not kept in motion, they would separate from it as they do in mines, where they are so destructive.

The savage, whose indolent habits are quite opposed to the practice of cleanliness, is never permitted to reside long in an unwholesome habitation. Insects, which our fastidious delicacy will scarcely venture to name, attack him; and, all untractable as he is to discipline, he is soon compelled by these "officers of health" to remove to another thicket, where he again breathes the fresh air of the woods, untainted by any noxious vapour. Together with the spices and stimulants of the East, the Europeans have imported the bug, which compels them to pay an increased attention to cleanliness, necessary, perhaps, to constitutions enfeebled by an increase of luxury. Whenever man neglects the dictates of nature, he is sure to be the sufferer. The awful dispensation by which we have been visited lately must have convinced every one who witnessed it, that they who reside in situations where those substances which make powerful manures are suffered to accumulate, are in a remarkable degree exposed to the attacks of pestilential diseases. It cannot yet be forgotten that the destructive fever introduced some years ago by an overcrowded cargo of emigrants was confined to the same parts of the town, and nearly to the same houses, that were most affected by the cholera. Believing such scourges to be the chastisements of a father, not less kind than just, and that they are not only never sent when not deserved, but also that they are always useful to the nations they visit, I shall (leaving those who are better qualified to notice the important moral instruction they convey) take some notice of the economical lesson which we ought to learn from what we have seen. A most destructive war had ravaged Europe for a long time. At its conclusion an immense body of men were dismissed to seek their support by their labour, after having learned no other trade than war, and being, of course, less qualified to succeed than if they had cultivated the arts of peace: the camp being always a poor school to teach industry, prudence, and economy. The enormous debts contracted during the war bear heavily upon all; and a greater, because constantly increasing, evil is to be found inhabits of unbounded luxury and extravagance, which have turned the labour of multitudes from producing the necessaries of life, to furnishing articles of luxury for a few very rich individuals. The pacific dispositions, or the empty treasuries, of the governments of Europe, have prevented any very extensive war for a considerable time; and there is a general complaint of the great and increasing distress of a superabundant population, who cannot find employment by which they can support themselves. This distress has reached such a height in our mother country, that opposite parties are predicting a bellum servile, or war of the servants against the masters; and it has been seriously proposed to enact laws to prevent a portion of the labouring class from marrying, by some wise men of that school which believes the earth to have been created, and to be governed, by chance; and who seem really to fear that it may fail to produce sufficient food for its inhabitants, if their wisdom should not interfere to lessen their numbers. At such a time as this, an unknown and new pestilential disease appears, which, baffling the skill of the physician, spreads from country to country, marking, by its victims, the situations where man has neglected accumulations of filth, which, applied to their proper use as manures, might have furnished employment and food for millions; and, at the same time, by the greater danger of a crowded situation, warning a portion of the inhabitants of thickly settled towns to remove to insulated situations in the country.

In every part of Europe manufactories appear to be increasing. The business is overdone; markets cannot be found sufficient to absorb the immense quantities of goods. The motive appears to be found in the great fortunes that some capitalists have acquired; for the condition of the operatives seems to be far from enviable, when compared with that of the agricultural labourer. It does appear to me that a warning has now been given to man, from a source of undoubted wisdom, to turn his attention more to agriculture. In no other employment is the labouring man more comfortable. Some trades require less exertion of bodily strength; but it is not the man who bears the most fatigue that is the least cheerful. It is not in the time that pestilential diseases are abroad only that an inattention to cleanliness is dangerous. I have so frequently observed scrofulous complaints in families that live in uncleanly situations, and particularly in those that inhabit rooms below the level of their yards, that I have long believed that chronic diseases may be induced by a greater than common proportion of irrespirable gases in the air. It has been observed in England, that in the parish workhouses there is an uncommon proportion of scrofula, rickets, and cutaneous diseases, among children. The necessaries of life are drawn principally from the culture of the earth. The annual labour produces the supply for the following season. Money, or what we call wealth, is the power of commanding this labour; but this power is not always wisely applied. From habit, men sometimes continue the business which formerly was profitable. That Being, who knows the failings of our nature, has, in kindness, made our provisions very perishable. Rats and mice, weevils and mites, mould and must, protect the poor from suffering by the avarice of the monopolist. He that possesses more food than he needs must soon dispose of it, or lose it. Like our provisions, the manures that are required to produce them must every season be applied to their proper use, if we would not expose ourselves both to loss and danger. A heap of manure, kept through the summer, loses much of its value; for in the hot season a part of it will take an aerial form, and pass through heaps of earth, which cannot contain aerial fluids; while, at the same time, the exhalations that rise from it endanger the health of those that reside near it. It appears, therefore, that, to preserve a wholesome air in our dwellings, we ought, previously to the hot season, to remove from their neighbourhood every thing that will serve for manure; and that, to render this manure most productive, it should be used immediately, and not reserved for a following season.

The accounts we so frequently receive of the distress of manufactories appear to prove that more hands are employed in them than there ought to be; but the accumulation of manures, that the cholera is constantly pointing out, do prove that agriculture is too much neglected. It is true that this language appears to be addressed to those who will never hear this lecture; but, as I believe it to be an important part of the lesson which has been given to the world, I have thought that it ought not to be passed over. Nor is it wholly irrelevant to ourselves, since, although few are employed inmanufactures, many among us, who might have supported themselves by agriculture, are now suffering from the failure of projects for acquiring wealth, in which they would not, perhaps, have engaged, but for the same disposition to follow the beaten track, and to trust to the supposed wisdom of others, which I have conceived may have led the inhabitants of Europe to push their manufactures too far. Nor is there, perhaps, any better mode of retrieving the consequences of our mistakes, than extending our agriculture, while we make our habitations more healthy, and raising greater quantities of provisions for exportation. Indeed, while the present difficulties continue, we may expect numbers to come to our shores from the land of our forefathers, whom I hope we may be always able to welcome to a country where food, at least, is cheap and abundant.